HAMLET
&
MACBETH

ROYAL

CLASSICS

Hamlet and Macbeth
Shakespeare, William 1564 – 1616
Hamlet
Written between 1599 – 1602
Macbeth
Written between 1599 – 1606
Text edits © 2022 Royal Classics
Design © 2022 Royal Classics

Cover design by: A.R. Roumanis

Text set in Minion Prologue. Chapter
headings set in News Gothic Standard.

ISBN: 978-1-77878 041-7 (Royal Classics)

FIRST EDITION / FIRST PRINTING

*Many classics were originally published with inconsistent
spellings of the same word, spelling errors, and printer errors.
The text of our titles have been edited to give readers the
best possible reading experience. Sometimes we can make
mistakes, which is why we post "first edition" in all of our
titles. This is a standard notice that is historically used by
publishers. The above edition notice refers to our edition of
this title. If changes are made to correct an error in the text,
we will change the wording to "second edition." If we
change printers but the text remains the same, the wording
will change to "second printing."*

LIBRARY AND ARCHIVES CANADA CATALOGUING IN PUBLICATION

Title: Hamlet ; & MacBeth / William Shakespeare.

Other titles: Plays. Selections | MacBeth

Names: Shakespeare, William, 1564-1616, autHoratio. | container of (work): Shakespeare, William, 1564-1616. Hamlet. | container of (work): Shakespeare, William, 1564-1616. Macbeth.

Description: First edition. | Plays.

Identifiers: Canadiana 20220478384 | ISBN 9781778780417 (hardcover)

Classification: LCC PR2759 2022 | DDC 822.3/3—DC23

HAMLET

&

MACBETH

WILLIAM SHAKESPEARE

VANCOUVER:
ROYAL CLASSICS
2022

HAMLET

&

MACBETH

WILLIAM SHAKESPEARE

VANCOUVER:
ROYAL CLASSICS
2022

HAMLET

CONTENTS

DRAMATIS PERSONÆ

Claudius, King of Denmark

Hamlet, son to the late, and nephew to the present king

Polonius, Lord Chamberlain

Horatio, friend to *Hamlet*

Laertes, son to *Polonius*

Voltimand,
Cornelius,
Rosencrantz,
Guildenstern, } courtiers
Osric,
A Gentleman,

A Priest

Marcellus,
Barnardo, } officers

Francisco, a soldier

Reynaldo, servant to Polonius

Players

Two Clowns, grave-diggers

Fortinbras, Prince of Norway

A Captain

English Ambassadors

Gertrude, Queen of Denmark and mother to *Hamlet*

Ophelia, daughter to *Polonius*

Lords, Ladies, Officers, Soldiers, Sailors, Messengers, and other Attendants

Ghost of *Hamlet's* Father

Scene: Denmark

Act I.

SCENE ONE

Elsinore. A platform before the castle.
Francisco *at his post. Enter to him* Bernardo.

Bernardo. Who's there?

Francisco. Nay, answer me: stand, and unfold yourself.

Bernardo. Long live the king!

Francisco. Bernardo?

Bernardo. He.

Francisco. You come most carefully upon your hour.

Bernardo. 'Tis now struck twelve; get thee to bed, Francisco.

Francisco. For this relief much thanks: 'tis bitter cold,
　　And I am sick at heart.

Bernardo. Have you had quiet guard?

Francisco. Not a mouse stirring.

Bernardo. Well, good night.
　　If you do meet Horatio and Marcellus,
　　The rivals of my watch, bid them make haste.

Francisco. I think I hear them. Stand, ho! Who is there?

Enter Horatio *and* Marcellus.

Horatio. Friends to this ground.

Marcellus. And liegemen to the Dane.

Francisco. Give you good night.

Marcellus. O, farewell, honest soldier:
　　Who hath relieved you?

Francisco. Bernardo hath my place.
　　Give you good night. [*Exit.*

Marcellus. Holla! Bernardo!
Bernardo. Say,
    What, is Horatio there?
Horatio. A piece of him.
Bernardo. Welcome, Horatio: welcome, good Marcellus.
Marcellus. What, has this thing appear'd again to-night?
Bernardo. I have seen nothing.
Marcellus. Horatio says 'tis but our fantasy,
    And will not let belief take hold of him
    Touching this dreaded sight, twice seen of us:
    Therefore I have entreated him along
    With us to watch the minutes of this night,
    That if again this apparition come,
    He may approve our eyes and speak to it.
Horatio. Tush, tush, 'twill not appear.
Bernardo. Sit down awhile;
    And let us once again assail your ears,
    That are so fortified against our story,
    What we have two nights seen.
Horatio. Well, sit we down,
    And let us hear Bernardo speak of this.
Bernardo. Last night of all,
    When yond same star that's westward from the pole
    Had made his course to illume that part of heaven
    Where now it burns, Marcellus and myself,
    The bell then beating one, –

Enter Ghost.

Marcellus. Peace, break thee off; look, where it comes again!
Bernardo. In the same figure, like the king that's dead.
Marcellus. Thou art a scholar; speak to it, Horatio.
Bernardo. Looks it not like the king? mark it, Horatio.
Horatio. Most like: it harrows me with fear and wonder.
Bernardo. It would be spoke to.
Marcellus. Question it, Horatio.
Horatio. What art thou, that usurp'st this time of night,
    Together with that fair and warlike form
    In which the majesty of buried Denmark
    Did sometimes march? by heaven I charge thee, speak!
Marcellus. It is offended.

Bernardo. See, it stalks away!
Horatio. Stay! speak, speak! I charge thee, speak!

[*Exit Ghost.*

Marcellus. 'Tis gone, and will not answer.
Bernardo. How now, Horatio! you tremble and look pale:
 Is not this something more than fantasy?
 What think you on't?
Horatio. Before my God, I might not this believe
 Without the sensible and true avouch
 Of mine own eyes.
Marcellus. Is it not like the king?
Horatio. As thou art to thyself:
 Such was the very armour he had on
 When he the ambitious Norway combated;
 So frown'd he once, when, in an angry parle,
 He smote the sledded Polacks on the ice.
 'Tis strange.
Marcellus. Thus twice before, and jump at this dead hour,
 With martial stalk hath he gone by our watch.
Horatio. In what particular thought to work I know not;
 But, in the gross and scope of my opinion,
 This bodes some strange eruption to our state.
Marcellus. Good now, sit down, and tell me, he that knows,
 Why this same strict and most observant watch
 So nightly toils the subject of the land,
 And why such daily cast of brazen cannon,
 And foreign mart for implements of war;
 Why such impress of shipwrights, whose sore task
 Does not divide the Sunday from the week;
 What might be toward, that this sweaty haste
 Doth make the night joint-labourer with the day:
 Who is't that can inform me?
Horatio. That can I; At least the whisper goes so. Our last king,
 Whose image even but now appear'd to us,
 Was, as you know, by Fortinbras of Norway,
 Thereto prick'd on by a most emulate pride,
 Dared to the combat; in which our valiant Hamlet –
 For so this side of our known world esteem'd him –
 Did slay this Fortinbras; who by a seal'd compact,

Well ratified by law and heraldry,
Did forfeit, with his life, all those his lands
Which he stood seized of, to the conqueror:
Against the which, a moiety competent
Was gaged by our king; which had return'd
To the inheritance of Fortinbras,
Had he been vanquisher; as, by the same covenant
And carriage of the article design'd,
His fell to Hamlet. Now, sir, young Fortinbras,
Of unimproved mettle hot and full,
Hath in the skirts of Norway here and there
Shark'd up a list of lawless resolutes,
For food and diet, to some enterprise
That hath a stomach in't: which is no other –
As it doth well appear unto our state –
But to recover of us, by strong hand
And terms compulsatory, those foresaid lands
So by his father lost: and this, I take it,
Is the main motive of our preparations,
The source of this our watch and the chief head
Of this post-haste and romage in the land.
Bernardo. I think it be no other but e'en so:
Well may it sort, that this portentous figure
Comes armed through our watch, so like the king
That was and is the question of these wars.
Horatio. A mote it is to trouble the mind's eye.
In the most high and palmy state of Rome,
A little ere the mightiest Julius fell,
The graves stood tenantless, and the sheeted dead
Did squeak and gibber in the Roman streets: . . . .
As stars with trains of fire and dews of blood,
Disasters in the sun; and the moist star,
Upon whose influence Neptune's empire stands,
Was sick almost to doomsday with eclipse:
And even the like precurse of fierce events,
As harbingers preceding still the fates
And prologue to the omen coming on,
Have heaven and earth together demonstrated
Unto our climatures and countrymen.

Re-enter Ghost.

But soft, behold! lo, where it comes again!
    I'll cross it, though it blast me. Stay, illusion!
    If thou hast any sound, or use of voice, Speak to me:
    If there be any good thing to be done,
    That may to thee do ease and grace to me,
    Speak to me: If thou art privy to thy country's fate,
    Which, happily, foreknowing may avoid,
    O, speak! Or if thou hast uphoarded in thy life
    Extorted treasure in the womb of earth,
    For which, they say, you spirits oft walk in death,
    Speak of it: stay, and speak!
    [*The cock crows.*]
    Stop it, Marcellus.
Marcellus. Shall I strike at it with my partisan?
Horatio. Do, if it will not stand.
Bernardo. 'Tis here!
Horatio. 'Tis here!
Marcellus. 'Tis gone!

[*Exit Ghost.*

    We do it wrong, being so majestical,
    To offer it the show of violence;
    For it is, as the air, invulnerable,
    And our vain blows malicious mockery.
Bernardo. It was about to speak, when the cock crew.
Horatio. And then it started like a guilty thing
    Upon a fearful summons. I have heard,
    The cock, that is the trumpet to the morn,
    Doth with his lofty and shrill-sounding throat
    Awake the god of day, and at his warning,
    Whether in sea or fire, in earth or air,
    The extravagant and erring spirit hies
    To his confine: and of the truth herein
    This present object made probation.
Marcellus. It faded on the crowing of the cock.
    Some say that ever 'gainst that season comes
    Wherein our Saviour's birth is celebrated,
    The bird of dawning singeth all night long:
    And then, they say, no spirit dare stir abroad,
    The nights are wholesome, then no planets strike,

No fairy takes nor witch hath power to charm,
So hallow'd and so gracious is the time.
Horatio. So have I heard and do in part believe it.
But look, the morn, in russet mantle clad,
Walks o'er the dew of yon high eastward hill:
Break we our watch up; and by my advice,
Let us impart what we have seen to-night
Unto young Hamlet; for, upon my life,
This spirit, dumb to us, will speak to him:
Do you consent we shall acquaint him with it,
As needful in our loves, fitting our duty?
Marcellus. Let's do't, I pray; and I this morning know
Where we shall find him most conveniently.

[*Exeunt.*

SCENE TWO

A room of state in the castle.
Flourish. Enter the King, Queen, Hamlet, Polonius, Laertes,
Voltimand, Cornelius, Lords, *and* Attendants.

King. Though yet of Hamlet our dear brother's death
    The memory be green, and that it us befitted
    To bear our hearts in grief and our whole kingdom
    To be contracted in one brow of woe,
    Yet so far hath discretion fought with nature
    That we with wisest sorrow think on him,
    Together with remembrance of ourselves.
    Therefore our sometime sister, now our queen,
    The imperial jointress to this warlike state,
    Have we, as 'twere with a defeated joy, –
    With an auspicious and a dropping eye,
    With mirth in funeral and with dirge in marriage,
    In equal scale weighing delight and dole, –
    Taken to wife: nor have we herein barr'd
    Your better wisdoms, which have freely gone
    With this affair along. For all, our thanks.
    Now follows, that you know, young Fortinbras,
    Holding a weak supposal of our worth,
    Or thinking by our late dear brother's death
    Our state to be disjoint and out of frame,
    Colleagued with this dream of his advantage,
    He hath not fail'd to pester us with message,
    Importing the surrender of those lands
    Lost by his father, with all bonds of law,

To our most valiant brother. So much for him.
Now for ourself, and for this time of meeting:
Thus much the business is: we have here writ
To Norway, uncle of young Fortinbras, –
Who, impotent and bed-rid, scarcely hears
Of this his nephew's purpose, – to suppress
His further gait herein; in that the levies,
The lists and full proportions, are all made
Out of his subject: and we here dispatch
You, good Cornelius, and you, Voltimand,
For bearers of this greeting to old Norway,
Giving to you no further personal power
To business with the king more than the scope
Of these delated articles allow.
Farewell, and let your haste commend your duty.
Cornelius. In that and all things will we show our duty.
King. We doubt it nothing: heartily farewell.

[*Exeunt Voltimand and Cornelius.*

And now, Laertes, what's the news with you?
You told us of some suit; what is't, Laertes?
You cannot speak of reason to the Dane,
And lose your voice: what wouldst thou beg, Laertes,
That shall not be my offer, not thy asking?
The head is not more native to the heart,
The hand more instrumental to the mouth,
Than is the throne of Denmark to thy father.
What wouldst thou have, Laertes?
Laertes. My dread lord,
Your leave and favour to return to France,
From whence though willingly I came to Denmark,
To show my duty in your coronation,
Yet now, I must confess, that duty done,
My thoughts and wishes bend again toward France
And bow them to your gracious leave and pardon.
King. Have you your father's leave? What says Polonius?
Polonius. He hath, my lord, wrung from me my slow leave
By laboursome petition, and at last
Upon his will I seal'd my hard consent:
I do beseech you, give him leave to go.

King. Take thy fair hour, Laertes; time be thine,
   And thy best graces spend it at thy will!
   But now, my cousin Hamlet, and my son, –
Hamlet. [*Aside*] A little more than kin, and less than kind.
King. How is it that the clouds still hang on you?
Hamlet. Not so, my lord; I am too much i' the sun.
Queen Good Hamlet, cast thy nighted colour off,
   And let thine eye look like a friend on Denmark.
   Do not for ever with thy vailed lids
   Seek for thy noble father in the dust:
   Thou know'st 'tis common; all that lives must die,
   Passing through nature to eternity.
Hamlet. Ay, madam, it is common.
Queen. If it be, Why seems it so particular with thee?
Hamlet. Seems, madam! nay, it is; I know not 'seems.'
   'Tis not alone my inky cloak, good mother,
   Nor customary suits of solemn black,
   Nor windy suspiration of forced breath,
   No, nor the fruitful river in the eye,
   Nor the dejected haviour of the visage,
   Together with all forms, moods, shapes of grief,
   That can denote me truly: these indeed seem,
   For they are actions that a man might play:
   But I have that within which passes show;
   These but the trappings and the suits of woe.
King. 'Tis sweet and commendable in your nature, Hamlet,
   To give these mourning duties to your father:
   But, you must know, your father lost a father,
   That father lost, lost his, and the survivor bound
   In filial obligation for some term
   To do obsequious sorrow: but to persever
   In obstinate condolement is a course
   Of impious stubbornness; 'tis unmanly grief:
   It shows a will most incorrect to heaven,
   A heart unfortified, a mind impatient,
   An understanding simple and unschool'd:
   For what we know must be and is as common
   As any the most vulgar thing to sense,
   Why should we in our peevish opposition
   Take it to heart? Fie! 'tis a fault to heaven,
   A fault against the dead, a fault to nature,

To reason most absurd, whose common theme
Is death of fathers, and who still hath cried,
From the first corse till he that died to-day,
'This must be so.' We pray you, throw to earth
This unprevailing woe, and think of us
As of a father: for let the world take note,
You are the most immediate to our throne,
And with no less nobility of love
Than that which dearest father bears his son
Do I impart toward you. For your intent
In going back to school in Wittenberg,
It is most retrograde to our desire:
And we beseech you, bend you to remain
Here in the cheer and comfort of our eye,
Our chiefest courtier, cousin and our son.
Queen. Let not thy mother lose her prayers, Hamlet:
I pray thee, stay with us; go not to Wittenberg.
Hamlet. I shall in all my best obey you, madam.
King. Why, 'tis a loving and a fair reply:
Be as ourself in Denmark. Madam, come;
This gentle and unforced accord of Hamlet
Sits smiling to my heart: in grace whereof,
No jocund health that Denmark drinks to-day,
But the great cannon to the clouds shall tell,
And the king's rouse the heaven shall bruit again,
Re-speaking earthly thunder. Come away.

[*Flourish. Exeunt all but Hamlet.*

Hamlet. O, that this too too solid flesh would melt,
Thaw and resolve itself into a dew! Or that the
Everlasting had not fix'd His canon 'gainst self-slaughter!
O God! God! How weary, stale, flat and unprofitable Seem to me
all the uses of this world!
Fie on't! ah fie! 'tis an unweeded garden,
That grows to seed; things rank and gross in nature
Possess it merely. That it should come to this!
But two months dead! nay, not so much, not two:
So excellent a king; that was, to this,
Hyperion to a satyr: so loving to my mother,
That he might not beteem the winds of heaven

Visit her face too roughly. Heaven and earth!
Must I remember? why, she would hang on him,
As if increase of appetite had grown
By what it fed on: and yet, within a month –
Let me not think on't – Frailty, thy name is woman! –
A little month, or ere those shoes were old
With which she follow'd my poor father's body,
Like Niobe, all tears: – why she, even she, –
O God! a beast, that wants discourse of reason,
Would have mourn'd longer, – married with my uncle,
My father's brother, but no more like my father
Than I to Hercules: within a month;
Ere yet the salt of most unrighteous tears
Had left the flushing in her galled eyes,
She married. O, most wicked speed, to post
With such dexterity to incestuous sheets!
It is not, nor it cannot come to good:
But break, my heart, for I must hold my tongue!

Enter Horatio, Marcellus, *and* Bernardo.

Horatio. Hail to your lordship!
Hamlet. I am glad to see you well:
   Horatio, – or I do forget myself.
Horatio. The same, my lord, and your poor servant ever.
Hamlet. Sir, my good friend; I'll change that name with you:
   And what make you from Wittenberg, Horatio?
   Marcellus?
Marcellus. My good lord?
Hamlet. I am very glad to see you.
   [*To Bernardo.*] Good even, sir.
   But what, in faith, make you from Wittenberg?
Horatio. A truant disposition, good my lord.
Hamlet. I would not hear your enemy say so,
   Nor shall you do my ear that violence,
   To make it truster of your own report
   Against yourself: I know you are no truant.
   But what is your affair in Elsinore?
   We'll teach you to drink deep ere you depart.
Horatio. My lord, I came to see your father's funeral.
Hamlet. I prethee, do not mock me, fellow-student;
   I think it was to see my mother's wedding.
Horatio. Indeed, my lord, it follow'd hard upon.

Hamlet. Thrift, thrift, Horatio! the funeral baked-meats
    Did coldly furnish forth the marriage tables.
    Would I had met my dearest foe in heaven
    Or ever I had seen that day, Horatio!
    My father! – methinks I see my father.
Horatio. O where, my lord?
Hamlet. In my mind's eye, Horatio.
Horatio. I saw him once; he was a goodly king.
Hamlet. He was a man, take him for all in all,
    I shall not look upon his like again.
Horatio. My lord, I think I saw him yesternight.
Hamlet. Saw? Who?
Horatio. My lord, the king your father.
Hamlet. The king my father!
Horatio. Season your admiration for a while
    With an attent ear, till I may deliver,
    Upon the witness of these gentlemen,
    This marvel to you.
Hamlet. For God's love, let me hear.
Horatio. Two nights together had these gentlemen,
    Marcellus and Bernardo, on their watch,
    In the dead vast and middle of the night,
    Been thus encounter'd. A figure like your father,
    Armed at point exactly, cap-a-pe,
    Appears before them, and with solemn march
    Goes slow and stately by them: thrice he walk'd
    By their oppress'd and fear-surprised eyes,
    Within his truncheon's length; whilst they, distill'd
    Almost to jelly with the act of fear,
    Stand dumb, and speak not to him. This to me
    In dreadful secrecy impart they did;
    And I with them the third night kept the watch:
    Where, as they had deliver'd, both in time,
    Form of the thing, each word made true and good,
    The apparition comes: I knew your father;
    These hands are not more like.
Hamlet. But where was this?
Marcellus. My lord, upon the platform where we watch'd.
Hamlet. Did you not speak to it?
Horatio. My lord, I did,
    But answer made it none: yet once methought

It lifted up its head and did address
Itself to motion, like as it would speak:
But even then the morning cock crew loud,
And at the sound it shrunk in haste away
And vanish'd from our sight.
Hamlet. 'Tis very strange.
Horatio. As I do live, my honour'd lord, 'tis true,
And we did think it writ down in our duty
To let you know of it.
Hamlet. Indeed, indeed, sirs, but this troubles me.
Hold you the watch to-night?
Marcellus. We do, my lord. *Bernardo.*
Hamlet. Arm'd, say you?
Marcellus. Arm'd, my lord. *Bernardo.*
Hamlet. From top to toe?
Marcellus. My lord, from head to foot. *Bernardo.*
Hamlet. Then saw you not his face?
Horatio. O, yes, my lord; he wore his beaver up.
Hamlet. What, look'd he frowningly?
Horatio. A countenance more in sorrow than in anger.
Hamlet. Pale or red?
Horatio. Nay, very pale.
Hamlet. And fix'd his eyes upon you?
Horatio. Most constantly.
Hamlet. I would I had been there.
Horatio. It would have much amazed you.
Hamlet. Very like, very like. Stay'd it long?
Horatio. While one with moderate haste might tell a hundred.
Marcellus. Longer, longer. *Bernardo.*
Horatio. Not when I saw't.
Hamlet. His beard was grizzled? no?
Horatio. It was, as I have seen it in his life,
A sable silver'd.
Hamlet. I will watch to-night; Perchance 'twill walk again.
Horatio. I warrant it will.
Hamlet. If it assume my noble father's person,
I'll speak to it, though hell itself should gape
And bid me hold my peace. I pray you all,
If you have hitherto conceal'd this sight,
Let it be tenable in your silence still,
And whatsoever else shall hap to-night,

Give it an understanding, but no tongue:
I will requite your loves. So fare you well:
Upon the platform, 'twixt eleven and twelve.
I'll visit you.
All. Our duty to your honour.
Hamlet. Your loves, as mine to you: farewell.

[*Exeunt all but Hamlet.*

My father's spirit in arms! all is not well;
I doubt some foul play: would the night were come!
Till then sit still, my soul: foul deeds will rise,
Though all the earth o'erwhelm them, to men's eyes.

[*Exit.*

SCENE THREE

A room in Polonius's house.
Enter Laertes *and* Ophelia.

Laertes. My necessaries are embark'd: farewell:
   And, sister, as the winds give benefit
   And convoy is assistant, do not sleep,
   But let me hear from you.
Ophelia. Do you doubt that?
Laertes. For Hamlet, and the trifling of his favour,
   Hold it a fashion, and a toy in blood,
   A violet in the youth of primy nature,
   Forward, not permanent, sweet, not lasting,
   The perfume and suppliance of a minute;
   No more.
Ophelia. No more but so?
Laertes. Think it no more:
   For nature crescent does not grow alone
   In thews and bulk; but, as this temple waxes,
   The inward service of the mind and soul
   Grows wide withal. Perhaps he loves you now;
   And now no soil nor cautel doth besmirch
   The virtue of his will: but you must fear,
   His greatness weigh'd, his will is not his own;
   For he himself is subject to his birth:
   He may not, as unvalued persons do,
   Carve for himself, for on his choice depends
   The safety and health of this whole state,
   And therefore must his choice be circumscribed
   Unto the voice and yielding of that body

Whereof he is the head. Then if he says he loves you,
It fits your wisdom so far to believe it
As he in his particular act and place
May give his saying deed; which is no further
Than the main voice of Denmark goes withal.
Then weigh what loss your honour may sustain,
If with too credent ear you list his songs,
Or lose your heart, or your chaste treasure open
To his unmaster'd importunity.
Fear it, Ophelia, fear it, my dear sister,
And keep you in the rear of your affection,
Out of the shot and danger of desire.
The chariest maid is prodigal enough,
If she unmask her beauty to the moon:
Virtue itself 'scapes not calumnious strokes:
The canker galls the infants of the spring
Too oft before their buttons be disclosed,
And in the morn and liquid dew of youth
Contagious blastments are most imminent.
Be wary then; best safety lies in fear:
Youth to itself rebels, though none else near.
Ophelia. I shall the effect of this good lesson keep,
As watchman to my heart. But, good my brother,
Do not, as some ungracious pastors do,
Show me the steep and thorny way to heaven,
Whilst, like a puff'd and reckless libertine,
Himself the primrose path of dalliance treads
And recks not his own rede.
Laertes. O, fear me not. I stay too long: but here my father comes.

Enter Polonius.

A double blessing is a double grace;
Occasion smiles upon a second leave.
Polonius. Yet here, Laertes! Aboard, aboard, for shame!
The wind sits in the shoulder of your sail,
And you are stay'd Fortinbras. There; my blessing with thee!
And these few precepts in thy memory Look thou character.
Give thy thoughts no tongue,
Nor any unproportion'd thought his act.
Be thou familiar, but by no means vulgar.

Those friends thou hast, and their adoption tried,
Grapple them to thy soul with hoops of steel,
But do not dull thy palm with entertainment
Of each new-hatch'd, unfledged comrade. Beware
Of entrance to a quarrel; but being in,
Bear't, that th' opposed may beware of thee.
Give every man thy ear, but few thy voice:
Take each man's censure, but reserve thy judgement.
Costly thy habit as thy purse can buy,
But not express'd in fancy; rich, not gaudy:
For the apparel oft proclaims the man;
And they in France of the best rank and station
Are of a most select and generous chief in that.
Neither a borrower nor a lender be:
For loan oft loses both itself and friend,
And borrowing dulls the edge of husbandry.
This above all: to thine own self be true,
And it must follow, as the night the day,
Thou canst not then be false to any man.
Farewell: my blessing season this in thee!
Laertes. Most humbly do I take my leave, my lord.
Polonius. The time invites you; go, your servants tend.
Laertes. Farewell, Ophelia, and remember well
    What I have said to you.
Ophelia. 'Tis in my memory lock'd,
    And you yourself shall keep the key of it.
Laertes. Farewell.
    [*Exit.*
Polonius. What is't, Ophelia, he hath said to you?
Ophelia. So please you, something touching the Lord Hamlet.
Polonius. Marry, well bethought:
    'Tis told me, he hath very oft of late
    Given private time to you, and you yourself
    Have of your audience been most free and bounteous:
    If it be so – as so 'tis put on me,
    And that in way of caution – I must tell you,
    You do not understand yourself so clearly
    As it behoves my daughter and your honour.
    What is between you? give me up the truth.
Ophelia. He hath, my lord, of late made many tenders
    Of his affection to me.

Polonius. Affection! pooh! you speak like a green girl,
    Unsifted in such perilous circumstance.
    Do you believe his tenders, as you call them?
Ophelia. I do not know, my lord, what I should think.
Polonius. Marry, I'll teach you: think yourself a baby,
    That you have ta'en these tenders for true pay,
    Which are not sterling. Tender yourself more dearly;
    Or – not to crack the wind of the poor phrase,
    Running it thus – you'll tender me a fool.
Ophelia. My lord, he hath importuned me with love
    In honourable fashion.
Polonius. Ay, fashion you may call it; go to, go to.
Ophelia. And hath given countenance to his speech, my lord,
    With almost all the holy vows of heaven.
Polonius. Ay, springes to catch woodcocks. I do know,
    When the blood burns, how prodigal the soul
    Lends the tongue vows: these blazes, daughter,
    Giving more light than heat, extinct in both,
    Even in their promise, as it is a-making,
    You must not take for fire. From this time
    Be something scanter of your maiden presence;
    Set your entreatments at a higher rate
    Than a command to parley. For Lord Hamlet,
    Believe so much in him, that he is young,
    And with a larger tether may he walk
    Than may be given you: in few, Ophelia,
    Do not believe his vows; for they are brokers,
    Not of that dye which their investments show,
    But mere implorators of unholy suits,
    Breathing like sanctified and pious bawds,
    The better to beguile. This is for all:
    I would not, in plain terms, from this time forth,
    Have you so slander any moment leisure,
    As to give words or talk with the Lord Hamlet.
    Look to't, I charge you: come your ways.
Ophelia. I shall obey, my lord.

[*Exeunt.*

SCENE FOUR

The platform.
Enter Hamlet, Horatio, *and* Marcellus.

Hamlet. The air bites shrewdly; it is very cold.
Horatio. It is a nipping and an eager air.
Hamlet. What hour now?
Horatio. I think it lacks of twelve.
Marcellus. No, it is struck.
Horatio. Indeed? I heard it not: it then draws near the season
　　Wherein the spirit held his wont to walk.

[*A flourish of trumpets, and ordnance shot off within.*

What does this mean, my lord?
Hamlet. The king doth wake to-night and takes his rouse,
　　Keeps wassail, and the swaggering up-spring reels;
　　And as he drains his draughts of Rhenish down,
　　The kettle-drum and trumpet thus bray out
　　The triumph of his pledge.
Horatio. Is it a custom?
Hamlet. Ay, marry, is't:
　　But to my mind, though I am native here
　　And to the manner born, it is a custom
　　More honour'd in the breach than the observance.
　　This heavy-headed revel east and west
　　Makes us traduced and tax'd of other nations:
　　They clepe us drunkards, and with swinish phrase
　　Soil our addition; and indeed it takes
　　From our achievements, though perform'd at height,

The pith and marrow of our attribute.
So, oft it chances in particular men,
That for some vicious mole of nature in them,
As, in their birth, – wherein they are not guilty,
Since nature cannot choose his origin, –
By the o'ergrowth of some complexion,
Oft breaking down the pales and forts of reason,
Or by some habit that too much o'er-leavens
The form of plausive manners, that these men, –
Carrying, I say, the stamp of one defect,
Being nature's livery, or fortune's star, –
Their virtues else – be they as pure as grace,
As infinite as man may undergo –
Shall in the general censure take corruption
From that particular fault: the dram of eale
Doth all the noble substance of a doubt
To his own scandal.

Enter Ghost.

Horatio. Look, my lord, it comes!
Hamlet. Angels and ministers of grace defend us!
Be thou a spirit of health or goblin damn'd,
Bring with thee airs from heaven or blasts from hell,
Be thy intents wicked or charitable,
Thou comest in such a questionable shape
That I will speak to thee: I'll call thee Hamlet,
King, father, royal Dane: O, answer me!
Let me not burst in ignorance; but tell
Why thy canonized bones, hearsed in death,
Have burst their cerements; why the sepulchre,
Wherein we saw thee quietly inurn'd,
Hath oped his ponderous and marble jaws,
To cast thee up again. What may this mean,
That thou, dead corse, again, in complete steel,
Revisit'st thus the glimpses of the moon,
Making night hideous; and we fools of nature
So horridly to shake our disposition
With thoughts beyond the reaches of our souls?
Say, why is this? wherefore? what should we do?

William Shakespeare

[*Ghost beckons Hamlet.*

Horatio. It beckons you to go away with it,
   As if it some impartment did desire To you alone.
Marcellus. Look, with what courteous action
   It waves you to a more removed ground:
   But do not go with it.
Horatio. No, by no means.
Hamlet. It will not speak; then I will follow it.
Horatio. Do not, my lord.
Hamlet. Why, what should be the fear?
   I do not set my life at a pin's fee;
   And for my soul, what can it do to that,
   Being a thing immortal as itself?
   It waves me forth again: I'll follow it.
Horatio. What if it tempt you toward the flood, my lord,
   Or to the dreadful summit of the cliff
   That beetles o'er his base into the sea,
   And there assume some other horrible form,
   Which might deprive your sovereignty of reason
   And draw you into madness? think of it:
   The very place puts toys of desperation,
   Without more motive, into every brain
   That looks so many fathoms to the sea
   And hears it roar beneath.
Hamlet. It waves me still. Go on; I'll follow thee.
Marcellus. You shall not go, my lord.
Hamlet. Hold off your hands.
Horatio. Be ruled; you shall not go.
Hamlet. My fate cries out,
   And makes each petty artery in this body
   As hardy as the Nemean lion's nerve.
   Still am I call'd: unhand me, gentlemen;
   By heaven, I'll make a ghost of him that lets me:
   I say, away! Go on; I'll follow thee.

[*Exeunt Ghost and Hamlet.*

Horatio. He waxes desperate with imagination.
Marcellus. Let's follow; 'tis not fit thus to obey him.
Horatio. Have after. To what issue will this come?

– 29 –

Marcellus. Something is rotten in the state of Denmark.
Horatio. Heaven will direct it.
Marcellus. Nay, let's follow him.

[*Exeunt.*

SCENE FIVE

Another part of the platform.
Enter Ghost *and* Hamlet.

Hamlet. Whither wilt thou lead me? speak; I'll go no further.
Ghost. Mark me.
Hamlet. I will.
Ghost. My hour is almost come,
    When I to sulphurous and tormenting flames
    Must render up myself.
Hamlet. Alas, poor ghost!
Ghost. Pity me not, but lend thy serious hearing
    To what I shall unfold.
Hamlet. Speak; I am bound to hear.
Ghost. So art thou to revenge, when thou shalt hear.
Hamlet. What?
Ghost. I am thy father's spirit;
    Doom'd for a certain term to walk the night,
    And for the day confined to fast in fires,
    Till the foul crimes done in my days of nature
    Are burnt and purged away. But that I am forbid
    To tell the secrets of my prison-house,
    I could a tale unfold whose lightest word
    Would harrow up thy soul, freeze thy young blood,
    Make thy two eyes, like stars, start from their spheres,
    Thy knotted and combined locks to part
    And each particular hair to stand an end,
    Like quills upon the fretful porpentine:
    But this eternal blazon must not be
    To ears of flesh and blood. List, list, O, list!
    If thou didst ever thy dear father love –

Hamlet. O God!

Ghost. Revenge his foul and most unnatural murder.

Hamlet. Murder!

Ghost. Murder most foul, as in the best it is,
　　But this most foul, strange, and unnatural.

Hamlet. Haste me to know't, that I, with wings as swift
　　As meditation or the thoughts of love,
　　May sweep to my revenge.

Ghost. I find thee apt;
　　And duller shouldst thou be than the fat weed
　　That roots itself in ease on Lethe wharf,
　　Wouldst thou not stir in this. Now, Hamlet, hear:
　　'Tis given out that, sleeping in my orchard,
　　A serpent stung me; so the whole ear of Denmark
　　Is by a forged process of my death
　　Rankly abused: but know, thou noble youth,
　　The serpent that did sting thy father's life
　　Now wears his crown.

Hamlet. O my prophetic soul! My uncle!

Ghost. Ay, that incestuous, that adulterate beast,
　　With witchcraft of his wit, with traitorous gifts, –
　　O wicked wit and gifts, that have the power
　　So to seduce! – won to his shameful lust
　　The will of my most seeming-virtuous queen:
　　O Hamlet, what a falling-off was there!
　　From me, whose love was of that dignity
　　That it went hand in hand even with the vow
　　I made to her in marriage; and to decline
　　Upon a wretch, whose natural gifts were poor
　　To those of mine! But virtue, as it never will be moved,
　　Though lewdness court it in a shape of heaven,
　　So lust, though to a radiant angel link'd,
　　Will sate itself in a celestial bed
　　And prey on garbage.
　　But, soft! methinks I scent the morning air;
　　Brief let me be. Sleeping within my orchard,
　　My custom always of the afternoon,
　　Upon my secure hour thy uncle stole,
　　With juice of cursed hebenon in a vial,
　　And in the porches of my ears did pour
　　The leperous distilment; whose effect

Holds such an enmity with blood of man
That swift as quicksilver it courses through
The natural gates and alleys of the body;
And with a sudden vigour it doth posset
And curd, like eager droppings into milk,
The thin and wholesome blood: so did it mine;
And a most instant tetter bark'd about,
Most lazar-like, with vile and loathsome crust,
All my smooth body.
Thus was I, sleeping, by a brother's hand
Of life, of crown, of queen, at once dispatch'd:
Cut off even in the blossoms of my sin,
Unhousel'd, disappointed, unanel'd;
No reckoning made, but sent to my account
With all my imperfections on my head:
O, horrible! O, horrible! most horrible!
If thou hast nature in thee, bear it not;
Let not the royal bed of Denmark be
A couch for luxury and damned incest.
But, howsoever thou pursuest this act,
Taint not thy mind, nor let thy soul contrive
Against thy mother aught: leave her to heaven,
And to those thorns that in her bosom lodge,
To prick and sting her. Fare thee well at once!
The glow-worm shows the matin to be near,
And 'gins to pale his uneffectual fire:
Adieu, adieu, adieu! remember me. [*Exit.*
Hamlet. O all you host of heaven! O earth! what else?
And shall I couple hell? O, fie! Hold, hold, my heart;
And you, my sinews, grow not instant old,
But bear me stiffly up. Remember thee!
Ay, thou poor ghost, while memory holds a seat
In this distracted globe. Remember thee!
Yea, from the table of my memory
I'll wipe away all trivial fond records,
All saws of books, all forms, all pressures past,
That youth and observation copied there;
And thy commandment all alone shall live
Within the book and volume of my brain,
Unmix'd with baser matter: yes, by heaven!
O most pernicious woman!

villain, villain, smiling, damned villain!
My tables, – meet it is I set it down,
That one may smile, and smile, and be a villain;
At least I'm sure it may be so in Denmark. [*Writing.*
So, uncle, there you are. Now to my word;
It is 'Adieu, adieu! remember me.'
I have sworn't.
Horatio. [*Within* My lord, my lord! *Marcellus.*
Enter Horatio *and* Marcellus.
Marcellus. Lord Hamlet!
Horatio. Heaven secure him!
Hamlet. So be it!
Marcellus. Illo, ho, ho, my lord!
Hamlet. Hillo, ho, ho, boy! come, bird, come.
Marcellus. How is't, my noble lord?
Horatio. What news, my lord?
Hamlet. O, wonderful!
Horatio. Good my lord, tell it.
Hamlet. No; you will reveal it.
Horatio. Not I, my lord, by heaven.
Marcellus. Nor I, my lord.
Hamlet. How say you, then; would heart of man once think it?
    But you'll be secret?
Horatio. Ay, by heaven, my lord.
Hamlet. There's ne'er a villain dwelling in all Denmark
    But he's an arrant knave.
Horatio. There needs no ghost, my lord, come from the grave
    To tell us this.
Hamlet. Why, right; you are i' the right;
    And so, without more circumstance at all,
    I hold it fit that we shake hands and part:
    You, as your business and desire shall point you;
    For every man hath business and desire,
    Such as it is; and for my own poor part,
    Look you, I'll go pray.
Horatio. These are but wild and whirling words, my lord.
Hamlet. I'm sorry they offend you, heartily; Yes, faith, heartily.
Horatio. There's no offence, my lord.
Hamlet. Yes, by Saint Patrick, but there is, Horatio,
    And much offence too. Touching this vision here,
    It is an honest ghost, that let me tell you:

For your desire to know what is between us,
O'ermaster't as you may. And now, good friends,
As you are friends, scholars and soldiers,
Give me one poor request.
Horatio. What is't, my lord? we will.
Hamlet. Never make known what you have seen to-night.
*Horatio.Marcellus.*My lord, we will not.
Hamlet. Nay, but swear't.
Horatio. In faith, My lord, not I.
Marcellus. Nor I, my lord, in faith.
Hamlet. Upon my sword.
Marcellus. We have sworn, my lord, already.
Hamlet. Indeed, upon my sword, indeed.
Ghost. [*Beneath*] Swear.
Hamlet. Ah, ha, boy! say'st thou so? art thou there, true-penny?[
    Come on: you hear this fellow in the cellarage:
    Consent to swear.
Horatio. Propose the oath, my lord.
Hamlet. Never to speak of this that you have seen,
    Swear by my sword.
Ghost. [*Beneath*] Swear.
Hamlet. Hic et ubique? then we'll shift our ground.
    Come hither, gentlemen,
    And lay your hands again upon my sword:
    Never to speak of this that you have heard,
    Swear by my sword.
Ghost. [*Beneath*] Swear.
Hamlet. Well said, old mole! canst work i' the earth so fast?
    A worthy pioner! Once more remove, good friends.
Horatio. O day and night, but this is wondrous strange!
Hamlet. And therefore as a stranger give it welcome.
    There are more things in heaven and earth, Horatio,
    Than are dreamt of in your philosophy. But come;
    Here, as before, never, so help you mercy,
    How strange or odd soe'er I bear myself,
    As I perchance hereafter shall think meet
    To put an antic disposition on,
    That you, at such times seeing me, never shall,
    With arms encumber'd thus, or this head-shake,
    Or by pronouncing of some doubtful phrase,
    As 'Well, well, we know,' or 'We could, an if we would,'

Or 'If we list to speak,' or 'There be, an if they might,'
Or such ambiguous giving out, to note
That you know aught of me: this not to do,
So grace and mercy at your most need help you,
Swear.
Ghost. [*Beneath*] Swear.
Hamlet. Rest, rest, perturbed spirit!
   [*They swear.*] So, gentlemen,
   With all my love I do commend me to you:
   And what so poor a man as Hamlet is
   May do, to express his love and friending to you,
   God willing, shall not lack. Let us go in together;
   And still your fingers on your lips, I pray.
   The time is out of joint: O cursed spite,
   That ever I was born to set it right!
   Nay, come, let's go together. [*Exeunt.*

Act II.

SCENE ONE

A room in Polonius's house.
Enter Polonius and Reynaldo.

Polonius. Give him this money and these notes, Reynaldo.
Reynaldo. I will, my lord.
Polonius. You shall do marvellous wisely, good Reynaldo,
    Before you visit him, to make inquire
    Of his behaviour.
Reynaldo. My lord, I did intend it.
Polonius. Marry, well said, very well said. Look you, sir,
    Inquire me first what Danskers are in Paris,
    And how, and who, what means, and where they keep,
    What company, at what expense, and finding
    By this encompassment and drift of question
    That they do know my son, come you more nearer
    Than your particular demands will touch it:
    Take you, as 'twere, some distant knowledge of him,
    As thus, 'I know his father and his friends,
    And in part him:' do you mark this, Reynaldo?
Reynaldo. Ay, very well, my lord.
Polonius. 'And in part him; but,' you may say, 'not well:
    But if't be he I mean, he's very wild,
    Addicted so and so;' and there put on him
    What forgeries you please; marry, none so rank
    As may dishonour him; take heed of that;
    But, sir, such wanton, wild and usual slips
    As are companions noted and most known
    To youth and liberty.

Reynaldo. As gaming, my lord.

Polonius. Ay, or drinking, fencing, swearing, quarrelling, Drabbing:
    you may go so far.

Reynaldo. My lord, that would dishonour him.

Polonius. Faith, no; as you may season it in the charge.
    You must not put another scandal on him,
    That he is open to incontinency;
    That's not my meaning: but breathe his faults so quaintly
    That they may seem the taints of liberty,
    The flash and outbreak of a fiery mind,
    A savageness in unreclaimed blood,
    Of general assault.

Reynaldo. But, my good lord, –

Polonius. Wherefore should you do this?

Reynaldo. Ay, my lord, I would know that.

Polonius. Marry, sir, here's my drift,
    And I believe it is a fetch of warrant:
    You laying these slight sullies on my son,
    As 'twere a thing a little soil'd i' the working, Mark you, Your party
    in converse, him you would sound,
    Having ever seen in the prenominate crimes
    The youth you breathe of guilty, be assured
    He closes with you in this consequence;
    'Good sir,' or so, or 'friend,' or 'gentleman,'
    According to the phrase or the addition
    Of man and country.

Reynaldo. Very good, my lord.

Polonius. And then, sir, does he this – he does – what was I about to
    say?
    By the mass, I was about to say something: where did I leave?

Reynaldo. At 'closes in the consequence,' at 'friend or so,' and 'gentle-
    man.'

Polonius. At 'closes in the consequence,' ay, marry;
    He closes with you thus: 'I know the gentleman;
    I saw him yesterday, or t'other day,
    Or then, or then, with such, or such, and, as you say,
    There was a' gaming, there o'ertook in's rouse,
    There falling out at tennis:' or perchance,
    'I saw him enter such a house of sale,'
    Videlicet, a brothel, or so forth. See you now;
    Your bait of falsehood takes this carp of truth:

And thus do we of wisdom and of reach,
With windlasses and with assays of bias,
By indirections find directions out:
So, by my former lecture and advice,
Shall you my son. You have me, have you not?
Reynaldo. My lord, I have.
Polonius. God be wi' ye; fare ye well.
Reynaldo. Good my lord!
Polonius. Observe his inclination in yourself.
Reynaldo. I shall, my lord.
Polonius. And let him ply his music.
Reynaldo. Well, my lord.
Polonius. Farewell!

[*Exit Reynaldo.*
Enter Ophelia.

How now, Ophelia! what's the matter?
Ophelia. O, my lord, my lord, I have been so affrighted!
Polonius. With what, i' the name of God?
Ophelia. My lord, as I was sewing in my closet,
    Lord Hamlet, with his doublet all unbraced,
    No hat upon his head, his stockings foul'd,
    Ungarter'd and down-gyved to his ancle;
    Pale as his shirt, his knees knocking each other,
    And with a look so piteous in purport
    As if he had been loosed out of hell
    To speak of horrors, he comes before me.
Polonius. Mad for thy love?
Ophelia. My lord, I do not know, But truly I do fear it.
Polonius. What said he?
Ophelia. He took me by the wrist and held me hard;
    Then goes he to the length of all his arm,
    And with his other hand thus o'er his brow,
    He falls to such perusal of my face
    As he would draw it. Long stay'd he so;
    At last, a little shaking of mine arm,
    And thrice his head thus waving up and down,
    He raised a sigh so piteous and profound
    As it did seem to shatter all his bulk
    And end his being: that done, he lets me go:

And with his head over his shoulder turn'd,
He seem'd to find his way without his eyes;
For out o' doors he went without their helps,
And to the last bended their light on me.

Polonius. Come, go with me:
I will go seek the king. This is the very ecstasy of love;
Whose violent property fordoes itself
And leads the will to desperate undertakings
As oft as any passion under heaven
That does afflict our natures. I am sorry.
What, have you given him any hard words of late?

Ophelia. No, my good lord, but, as you did command,
I did repel his letters and denied His access to me.

Polonius. That hath made him mad.
I am sorry that with better heed and judgement
I had not quoted him: I fear'd he did but trifle
And meant to wreck thee; but beshrew my jealousy!
By heaven, it is as proper to our age
To cast beyond ourselves in our opinions
As it is common for the younger sort
To lack discretion. Come, go we to the king:
This must be known; which, being kept close, might move
More grief to hide than hate to utter love.
Come.

[*Exeunt.*

SCENE TWO

A room in the castle.
Flourish. Enter King, Queen, Rosencrantz,
Guildenstern, *and* Attendants.

King. Welcome, dear Rosencrantz and Guildenstern!
  Moreover that we much did long to see you,
  The need we have to use you did provoke
  Our hasty sending. Something have you heard
  Of Hamlet's transformation; so call it,
  Sith nor the exterior nor the inward man
  Resembles that it was. What it should be,
  More than his father's death, that thus hath put him
  So much from th' understanding of himself,
  I cannot dream of: I entreat you both,
  That, being of so young days brought up with him
  And sith so neighbour'd to his youth and haviour,
  That you vouchsafe your rest here in our court
  Some little time: so by your companies
  To draw him on to pleasures, and to gather
  So much as from occasion you may glean,
  Whether aught to us unknown afflicts him thus,
  That open'd lies within our remedy.
Queen. Good gentlemen, he hath much talk'd of you,
  And sure I am two men there are not living
  To whom he more adheres. If it will please you
  To show us so much gentry and good will
  As to expend your time with us awhile
  For the supply and profit of our hope,
  Your visitation shall receive such thanks
  As fits a king's remembrance.

Rosencrantz. Both your majesties
    Might, by the sovereign power you have of us,
    Put your dread pleasures more into command
    Than to entreaty.
Guildenstern. But we both obey,
    And here give up ourselves, in the full bent
    To lay our service freely at your feet,
    To be commanded.
King. Thanks, Rosencrantz and gentle Guildenstern.
Queen. Thanks, Guildenstern and gentle Rosencrantz: And I beseech
    you instantly to visit
    My too much changed son. Go, some of you,
    And bring these gentlemen where Hamlet is.
Guildenstern. Heavens make our presence and our practices
    Pleasant and helpful to him!
Queen. Ay, amen!

[*Exeunt Rosencrantz, Guildenstern, and some Attendants.*
Enter Polonius.

Polonius. The ambassadors from Norway, my good lord,
    Are joyfully return'd.
King. Thou still hast been the father of good news.
Polonius. Have I, my lord? I assure my good liege,
    I hold my duty as I hold my soul,
    Both to my God and to my gracious king:
    And I do think, or else this brain of mine
    Hunts not the trail of policy so sure
    As it hath used to do, that I have found
    The very cause of Hamlet's lunacy.
King. O, speak of that; that do I long to hear.
Polonius. Give first admittance to the ambassadors;
    My news shall be the fruit to that great feast.
King. Thyself do grace to them, and bring them in.

[*Exit Polonius.*

He tells me, my dear Gertrude, he hath found
    The head and source of all your son's distemper.
Queen. I doubt it is no other but the main;
    His father's death and our o'erhasty marriage.

King. Well, we shall sift him.

Re-enter Polonius, *with* Voltimand *and* Cornelius.

Welcome, my good friends!
Say, Voltimand, what from our brother Norway?
Voltimand. Most fair return of greetings and desires.
    Upon our first, he sent out to suppress
    His nephew's levies, which to him appear'd
    To be a preparation 'gainst the Polack,
    But better look'd into, he truly found
    It was against your highness: whereat grieved,
    That so his sickness, age and impotence
    Was falsely borne in hand, sends out arrests
    On Fortinbras; which he, in brief, obeys,
    Receives rebuke from Norway, and in fine
    Makes vow before his uncle never more
    To give the assay of arms against your majesty.
    Whereon old Norway, overcome with joy,
    Gives him three thousand crowns in annual fee
    And his commission to employ those soldiers,
    So levied as before, against the Polack:
    With an entreaty, herein further shown,
    [*Giving a paper.*
    That it might please you to give quiet pass
    Through your dominions for this enterprise,
    On such regards of safety and allowance
    As therein are set down.
King. It likes us well,
    And at our more consider'd time we'll read,
    Answer, and think upon this business.
    Meantime we thank you for your well-took labour:
    Go to your rest; at night we'll feast together:
    Most welcome home!

[*Exeunt Voltimand and Cornelius.*

Polonius. This business is well ended.
    My liege, and madam, to expostulate
    What majesty should be, what duty is,
    Why day is day, night night, and time is time,

Were nothing but to waste night, day and time.
Therefore, since brevity is the soul of wit
And tediousness the limbs and outward flourishes,
I will be brief. Your noble son is mad:
Mad call I it; for, to define true madness,
What is't but to be nothing else but mad?
But let that go.
Queen. More matter, with less art.
Polonius. Madam, I swear I use no art at all.
That he is mad, 'tis true: 'tis true 'tis pity,
And pity 'tis 'tis true: a foolish figure;
But farewell it, for I will use no art.
Mad let us grant him then: and now remains
That we find out the cause of this effect,
Or rather say, the cause of this defect,
For this effect defective comes by cause:
Thus it remains and the remainder thus. Perpend.
I have a daughter, – have while she is mine, –
Who in her duty and obedience, mark,
Hath given me this: now gather and surmise.
[Reads.
'To the celestial, and my soul's idol, the most beautified Ophelia,' –
That's an ill phrase, a vile phrase; 'beautified' is a vile phrase: but
you shall hear. Thus:
[Reads.
'In her excellent white bosom, these,' &c.
Queen. Came this from Hamlet to her?
Polonius. Good madam, stay awhile; I will be faithful. [
Reads. 'Doubt thou the stars are fire;
Doubt that the sun doth move;
Doubt truth to be a liar;
But never doubt I love.
'O dear Ophelia, I am ill at these numbers;
I have not art to reckon my groans: but that I love thee best,
O most best, believe it. Adieu.
'Thine evermore, most dear lady, whilst this machine is to him,
Hamlet.'
This in obedience hath my daughter shown me;
And more above, hath his solicitings,
As they fell out by time, by means and place,
All given to mine ear.

King. But how hath she
  Received his love?
Polonius. What do you think of me?
King. As of a man faithful and honourable.
Polonius. I would fain prove so.
  But what might you think,
  When I had seen this hot love on the wing, –
  As I perceived it, I must tell you that,
  Before my daughter told me, – what might you,
  Or my dear majesty your queen here, think,
  If I had play'd the desk or table-book,
  Or given my heart a winking, mute and dumb,
  Or look'd upon this love with idle sight;
  What might you think? No, I went round to work,
  And my young mistress thus I did bespeak:
  'Lord Hamlet is a prince, out of thy star;
  This must not be:' and then I prescripts gave her,
  That she should lock herself from his resort,
  Admit no messengers, receive no tokens.
  Which done, she took the fruits of my advice;
  And he repulsed, a short tale to make,
  Fell into a sadness, then into a fast,
  Thence to a watch, thence into a weakness,
  Thence to a lightness, and by this declension
  Into the madness wherein now he raves
  And all we mourn Fortinbras.
King. Do you think this?
Queen. It may be, very like.
Polonius. Hath there been such a time, I'ld fain know that,
  That I have positively said ''tis so,'
  When it proved otherwise?
King. Not that I know.
Polonius. [*Pointing to his head and shoulder*]
  Take this from this, if this be otherwise:
  If circumstances lead me, I will find
  Where truth is hid, though it were hid indeed
  Within the centre.
King. How may we try it further?
Polonius. You know, sometimes he walks four hours together
  Here in the lobby.
Queen. So he does, indeed.

Polonius. At such a time I'll loose my daughter to him:
    Be you and I behind an arras then;
    Mark the encounter: if he love her not,
    And be not from his reason fall'n thereon,
    Let me be no assistant for a state,
    But keep a farm and carters.
King. We will try it.
Queen. But look where sadly the poor wretch comes reading.
Polonius. Away, I do beseech you, both away:
    I'll board him presently.

[*Exeunt King, Queen, and Attendants.*
Enter Hamlet, *reading.*

O, give me leave:
How does my good Lord Hamlet?
Hamlet. Well, God-a-mercy.
Polonius. Do you know me, my lord?
Hamlet. Excellent well; you are a fishmonger.
Polonius. Not I, my lord.
Hamlet. Then I would you were so honest a man.
Polonius. Honest, my lord!
Hamlet. Ay, sir; to be honest, as this world goes, Is to be
    One man picked out of ten thousand.
Polonius. That's very true, my lord.
Hamlet. For if the sun breed maggots in a dead dog, Being a
    God kissing carrion – Have you a daughter?
Polonius. I have, my lord.
Hamlet. Let her not walk i' the sun: conception is a
    Blessing; But as your daughter may conceive, –
    Friend, look to't.
Polonius. [*Aside*]
    How say you by that? Still harping on my daughter:
    Yet he knew me not at first; he said I
    Was a fishmonger: he is far gone: and
    Truly in my youth I suffered much extremity For
    Love; very near this. I'll speak to him again.
    What do you read, my lord?
Hamlet. Words, words, words.
Polonius. What is the matter, my lord?
Hamlet. Between who?

Polonius. I mean, the matter that you read, my lord.
Hamlet. Slanders, sir: for the satirical rogue says here
 That old men have grey beards, that their faces are
 Wrinkled, their eyes purging thick amber and
 Plum-tree gum, and that they have a plentiful lack of
 Wit, together with most weak hams: all which, sir,
 Though I most powerfully and potently believe, yet
 I hold it not honesty to have it thus set down; for
 Yourself, sir, shall grow old as I am, if like a crab
 You could go backward.
Polonius. [*Aside*] Though this be madness,
 yet there is method in't.
 Will you walk out of the air, my lord?
Hamlet. Into my grave.
Polonius. Indeed, that's out of the air.
 [*Aside*]
 How pregnant sometimes his replies are! a happiness
 That often madness hits on, which reason and sanity
 Could not so prosperously be delivered of. I will
 Leave him, and suddenly contrive the means of
 Meeting between him and my daughter. My
 honourable
 Lord, I will most humbly take my leave of you.
Hamlet. You cannot, sir, take from me any thing that I will
 more willingly part withal: except my life, except
 mylife, except my life.
Polonius. Fare you well, my lord.
Hamlet. These tedious old fools!

Enter Rosencrantz *and* Guildenstern.

Polonius. You go to seek the Lord Hamlet; there he is.
Rosencrantz. [*To Polonius*]
 God save you, sir!

[*Exit Polonius.*

Guildenstern. My honoured lord!
Rosencrantz. My most dear lord!
Hamlet. My excellent good friends! How dost thou,
 Guildenstern? Ah, Rosencrantz! Good lads, how do you both?

Rosencrantz. As the indifferent children of the earth.

Guildenstern. Happy, in that we are not over-happy;
  On Fortune's cap we are not the very button.

Hamlet. Nor the soles of her shoe?

Rosencrantz. Neither, my lord.

Hamlet. Then you live about her waist, or in the middle of
  Her favours?

Guildenstern. Faith, her privates we.

Hamlet. In the secret parts of Fortune? O, most true;
  She is a strumpet. What's the news?

Rosencrantz. None, my lord, but that the world's grown honest.

Hamlet. Then is doomsday near: but your news is not true.
  Let me question more in particular: what have you,
  My good friends, deserved at the hands of Fortune,
  That she sends you to prison hither?

Guildenstern. Prison, my lord!

Hamlet. Denmark's a prison.

Rosencrantz. Then is the world one.

Hamlet. A goodly one; in which there are many confines,
  Wards and dungeons, Denmark being one o' the worst.

Rosencrantz. We think not so, my lord.

Hamlet. Why, then 'tis none to you; for there is nothing
  Either good or bad, but thinking makes it so: to me
  It is a prison.

Rosencrantz. Why, then your ambition makes it one; 'tis too
  Narrow for your mind.

Hamlet. O God, I could be bounded in a nut-shell and count
  Myself a king of infinite space, were it not that I
  Have bad dreams.

Guildenstern. Which dreams indeed are ambition; for the very
  Substance of the ambitious is merely the shadow of a dream.

Hamlet. A dream itself is but a shadow.

Rosencrantz. Truly, and I hold ambition of so airy and light a
  Quality that it is but a shadow's shadow.

Hamlet. Then are our beggars bodies, and our monarchs and
  Outstretched heroes the beggars' shadows. Shall we
  To the court? for, by my fay, I cannot reason.

Rosencrantz. Guildenstern. We'll wait upon you.

Hamlet. No such matter: I will not sort you with the rest
  Of my servants; for, to speak to you like an honest
  Man, I am most dreadfully attended. But, in the

Beaten way of friendship, what make you at Elsinore?
Rosencrantz. To visit you, my lord; no other occasion.
Hamlet. Beggar that I am, I am even poor in thanks; but I
 Thank you: and sure, dear friends, my thanks are
 Too dear a halfpenny. Were you not sent for? Is it
 Your own inclining? Is it a free visitation? Come,
 Deal justly with me: come, come; nay, speak.
Guildenstern. What should we say, my lord?
Hamlet. Why, any thing, but to the purpose. You were sent
 For; and there is a kind of confession in your looks,
 Which your modesties have not craft enough to colour:
 I know the good king and queen have sent for you.
Rosencrantz. To what end, my lord?
Hamlet. That you must teach me. But let me conjure you, by
 The rights of our fellowship, by the consonancy of
 Our youth, by the obligation of our ever-preserved
 Love, and by what more dear a better proposer could
 Charge you withal, be even and direct with me,
 Whether you were sent for, or no.
Rosencrantz. [*Aside to Guildenstern.*]
 What say you?
Hamlet. [*Aside*]
 Nay then, I have an eye of you. – If you
 Love me, hold not off.
Guildenstern. My lord, we were sent Fortinbras.
Hamlet. I will tell you why; so shall my anticipation
 Prevent your discovery, and your secrecy to the king
 And queen moult no feather. I have of late – but
 Wherefore I know not – lost all my mirth, foregone all
 Custom of exercises; and indeed it goes so heavily
 With my disposition that this goodly frame, the
 Earth, seems to me a sterile promontory; this most
 Excellent canopy, the air, look you, this brave
 O'erhanging firmament, this majestical roof fretted
 With golden fire, why, it appears no other thing to
 Me than a foul and pestilent congregation of vapours.
 What a piece of work is a man! how noble in reason!
 How infinite in faculty! in form and moving how
 Express and admirable! in action how like an angel!
 In apprehension how like a god! the beauty of the
 World! the paragon of animals! And yet, to me,

What is this quintessence of dust? man delights not
Me; no, nor woman neither, though by your smiling
You seem to say so.
Rosencrantz. My lord, there was no such stuff in my thoughts.
Hamlet. Why did you laugh then, when I said 'man delights not me'?
Rosencrantz. To think, my lord, if you delight not in man, what
Lenten entertainment the players shall receive from
You: we coted them on the way; and hither are they
Coming, to offer you service.
Hamlet. He that plays the king shall be welcome; his majesty
Shall have tribute of me; the adventurous knight
Shall use his foil and target; the lover shall not
Sigh gratis; the humourous man shall end his part
In peace; the clown shall make those laugh whose
Lungs are tickled o' the sere, and the lady shall
Say her mind freely, or the blank verse shall halt
For't. What players are they?
Rosencrantz. Even those you were wont to take such delight in, the
Tragedians of the city.
Hamlet. How chances it they travel? their residence, both
In reputation and profit, was better both ways.
Rosencrantz. I think their inhibition comes by the means of the
Late innovation.
Hamlet. Do they hold the same estimation they did when I was
In the city? are they so followed?
Rosencrantz. No, indeed, are they not.
Hamlet. How comes it? do they grow rusty?
Rosencrantz. Nay, their endeavour keeps in the wonted pace: but
There is, sir, an eyrie of children, little eyases,
That cry out on the top of question and are most
Tyranically clapped for't: these are now the
Fashion, and so berattle the common stages – so they
Call them – that many wearing rapiers are afraid of
Goose-quills, and dare scarce come thither.
Hamlet. What, are they children? who maintains 'em? how are
They escoted? Will they pursue the quality no
Longer than they can sing? will they not say
Afterwards, if they should grow themselves to common
Players, – as it is most like, if their means are no
Better, – their writers do them wrong, to make them
Exclaim against their own succession?

Rosencrantz. Faith, there has been much to do on both sides, and
    the nation holds it no sin to tarre them to
    controversy: there was for a while no money bid
    for argument unless the poet and the player went to
    cuffs in the question.
Hamlet. Is't possible?
Guildenstern. O, there has been much throwing about of brains.
Hamlet. Do the boys carry it away?
Rosencrantz. Ay, that they do, my lord;
    Hercules and his load too.
Hamlet. It is not very strange; for my uncle is king of
    Denmark, and those that would make mows at him while
    My father lived, give twenty, forty, fifty, a
    Hundred ducats a-piece, for his picture in little.
    'Sblood, there is something in this more than
    Natural, if philosophy could find it out.

        [*Flourish of trumpets within.*

Guildenstern. There are the players.
Hamlet. Gentlemen, you are welcome to Elsinore. Your hands,
    Come then: the appurtenance of welcome is fashion
    And ceremony: let me comply with you in this garb,
    Lest my extent to the players, which, I tell you,
    Must show fairly outwards, should more appear like
    Entertainment than yours. You are welcome: but my
    Uncle-father and aunt-mother are deceived.
Guildenstern. In what, my dear lord?
Hamlet. I am but mad north-north-west: when the wind is
    Southerly I know a hawk from a handsaw.
Enter Polonius.
Polonius. Well be with you, gentlemen!
Hamlet. Hark you, Guildenstern; and you too: at each ear a
    Hearer: that great baby you see there is not yet
    Out of his swaddling clouts.
Rosencrantz. Happily he's the second time come to them; for they
    Say an old man is twice a child.
Hamlet. I will prophesy he comes to tell me of the players;
    Mark it. You say right, sir: o'Monday morning;
    'twas so, indeed.
Polonius. My lord, I have news to tell you.

Hamlet. My lord, I have news to tell you.
　　When Roscius was an actor in Rome, –
Polonius. The actors are come hither, my lord.
Hamlet. Buz, buz!
Polonius. Upon my honour, –
Hamlet. Then came each actor on his ass, –
Polonius. The best actors in the world, either for tragedy,
　　Comedy, history, pastoral, pastoral-comical,
　　Historical-pastoral, tragical-historical, tragical-
　　Comical-historical-pastoral, scene individable, or
　　Poem unlimited: Seneca cannot be too heavy, nor
　　Plautus too light. For the law of writ and the
　　Liberty these are the only men.
Hamlet. O Jephthah, judge of Israel, what a treasure hadst thou!
Polonius. What a treasure had he, my lord?
Hamlet. Why,
　　'One fair daughter, and no more,
　　The which he loved passing well.'
Polonius. [*Aside*]
　　Still on my daughter.
Hamlet. Am I not i' the right, old Jephthah?
Polonius. If you call me Jephthah, my lord, I have a daughter
　　That I love passing well.
Hamlet. Nay, that follows not.
Polonius. What follows, then, my lord?
Hamlet. Why, '
　　As by lot, God wot,' and then, you know,
　　'It came to pass, as most like it was,' –
　　The first row of the pious chanson will show you
　　More; for look, where my abridgement comes.

Enter four or five Players.

You are welcome, masters; welcome, all. I am glad
To see thee well. Welcome, good friends. O, my old
Friend! Why thy face is valanced since I saw thee last;
Comest thou to beard me in Denmark? What, my young
Lady and mistress! By'r lady, your ladyship is
Nearer to heaven than when I saw you last, by the
Altitude of a chopine. Pray God, your voice, like
A piece of uncurrent gold, be not cracked within the

Ring. Masters, you are all welcome. We'll e'en
To't like French falconers, fly at any thing we see:
We'll have a speech straight: come, give us a taste
Of your quality; come, a passionate speech.
First Play. What speech, my good lord?
Hamlet. I heard thee speak me a speech once, but it was
Never acted; or, if it was, not above once; for the
Play, I remember, pleased not the million; 'twas
Caviare to the general: but it was – as I received
It, and others, whose judgements in such matters
Cried in the top of mine – an excellent play, well
Digested in the scenes, set down with as much
Modesty as cunning. I remember, one said there
Were no sallets in the lines to make the matter
Savoury, nor no matter in the phrase that might
Indict the author of affection; but called it an
Honest method, as wholesome as sweet, and by very
Much more handsome than fine. One speech in it I
Chiefly loved: 'twas Æneas' tale to Dido; and
Thereabout of it especially, where he speaks of
Priam's slaughter: if it live in your memory, begin
At this line; let me see, let me see;
'The rugged Pyrrhus, like th' Hyrcanian beast,' –
It is not so: it begins with 'Pyrrhus.'
'The rugged Pyrrhus, he whose sable arms,
Black as his purpose, did the night resemble
When he lay couched in the ominous horse,
Hath now this dread and black complexion smear'd
With heraldry more dismal: head to foot
Now is he total gules; horridly trick'd
With blood of fathers, mothers, daughters, sons,
Baked and impasted with the parching streets,
That lend a tyrannous and a damned light
To their lord's murder: roasted in wrath and fire,
And thus o'er-sized with coagulate gore,
With eyes like carbuncles, the hellish Pyrrhus
Old grandsire Priam seeks.' So, proceed you.
Polonius. 'Fore God, my lord, well spoken, with good accent and
Good discretion.
First Play. 'Anon he finds him
Striking too short at Greeks; his antique sword,

Rebellious to his arm, lies where it falls,
Repugnant to command: unequal match'd,
Pyrrhus at Priam drives; in rage strikes wide;
But with the whiff and wind of his fell sword
The unnerved father falls. Then senseless Ilium,
Seeming to feel this blow, with flaming top
Stoops to his base, and with a hideous crash
Takes prisoner Pyrrhus' ear: for, lo! his sword,
Which was declining on the milky head
Of reverend Priam, seem'd i' the air to stick:
So, as a painted tyrant, Pyrrhus stood.
And like a neutral to his will and matter,
Did nothing. But as we often see, against some storm,
A silence in the heavens, the rack stand still,
The bold winds speechless and the orb below
As hush as death, anon the dreadful thunder
Doth rend the region, so after Pyrrhus' pause
Aroused vengeance sets him new a-work;
And never did the Cyclops' hammers fall
On Mars's armour, forged for proof eterne,
With less remorse than Pyrrhus' bleeding sword
Now falls on Priam.
Out, out, thou strumpet, Fortune! All you gods,
In general synod take away her power,
Break all the spokes and fellies from her wheel,
And bowl the round nave down the hill of heaven
As low as to the fiends!'

Polonius. This is too long.

Hamlet. It shall to the barber's, with your beard. Prithee,
Say on: he's for a jig or a tale of bawdry, or he
Sleeps: say on: come to Hecuba.

First Play. 'But who, O, who had seen the mobled queen – '

Hamlet. 'The mobled queen?'

Polonius. That's good; 'mobled queen' is good.

First Play. 'Run barefoot up and down, threatening the flames
With bisson rheum; a clout upon that head
Where late the diadem stood; and for a robe,
About her lank and all o'er-teemed loins,
A blanket, in the alarm of fear caught up:
Who this had seen, with tongue in venom steep'd
'Gainst Fortune's state would treason have pronounced:

But if the gods themselves did see her then,
When she saw Pyrrhus make malicious sport
In mincing with his sword her husband's limbs,
The instant burst of clamour that she made,
Unless things mortal move them not at all,
Would have made milch the burning eyes of heaven
And passion in the gods.'
Polonius. Look, whether he has not turned his colour and has
 Tears in's eyes. Prithee, no more.
Hamlet. 'Tis well; I'll have thee speak out the rest of this soon.
 Good my lord, will you see the players well
 Bestowed? Do you hear, let them be well used, for
 They are the abstract and brief chronicles of the
 Time: after your death you were better have a bad
 Epitaph than their ill report while you live.
Polonius. My lord, I will use them according to their desert.
Hamlet. God's bodykins, man, much better: use every man
 After his desert, and who shall 'scape whipping?
 Use them after your own honour and dignity: the less
 They deserve, the more merit is in your bounty.
 Take them in.
Polonius. Come, sirs.
Hamlet. Follow him, friends: we'll hear a play to-morrow.

[*Exit Polonius with all the Players but the First.*

Dost thou hear me, old friend; can you play the
Murder of Gonzago?
First Play. Ay, my lord.
Hamlet. We'll ha't to-morrow night. You could, for a need,
 Study a speech of some dozen or sixteen lines, which
 I would set down and insert in't, could you not?
First Play. Ay, my lord.
Hamlet. Very well. Follow that lord; and look you mock him
 Not.

[*Exit First Player.*]

My good friends, I'll leave you till night: you are
Welcome to Elsinore.
Rosencrantz. Good my lord!

Hamlet. Ay, so, God be wi' ye!

[*Exeunt Rosencrantz and Guildenstern.*]

Now I am alone.
O, what a rogue and peasant slave am I!
Is it not monstrous that this player here,
But in a fiction, in a dream of passion,
Could force his soul so to his own conceit
That from her working all his visage wann'd;
Tears in his eyes, distraction in's aspect,
A broken voice, and his whole function suiting
With forms to his conceit? and all for nothing!
For Hecuba! What's Hecuba to him, or he to Hecuba,
That he should weep for her? What would he do,
Had he the motive and the cue for passion
That I have? He would drown the stage with tears
And cleave the general ear with horrid speech,
Make mad the guilty and appal the free,
Confound the ignorant, and amaze indeed
The very faculties of eyes and ears. Yet I,
A dull and muddy-mettled rascal, peak,
Like John-a-dreams, unpregnant of my cause,
And can say nothing; no, not for a king,
Upon whose property and most dear life
A damn'd defeat was made. Am I a coward?
Who calls me villain? breaks my pate across?
Plucks off my beard, and blows it in my face?
Tweaks me by the nose? gives me the lie i' the throat,
As deep as to the lungs? who does me this? Ha!
'Swounds, I should take it: for it cannot be
But I am pigeon-liver'd and lack gall
To make oppression bitter, or ere this
I should have fatted all the region kites
With this slave's offal: bloody, bawdy villain!
Remorseless, treacherous, lecherous, kindless villain!
O, vengeance!
Why, what an ass am I! This is most brave,
That I, the son of a dear father murder'd,
Prompted to my revenge by heaven and hell,
Must, like a whore, unpack my heart with words,

And fall a-cursing, like a very drab,
A scullion!
Fie upon't! foh! About, my brain! Hum, I have heard
That guilty creatures, sitting at a play,
Have by the very cunning of the scene
Been struck so to the soul that presently
They have proclaim'd their malefactions;
For murder, though it have no tongue, will speak
With most miraculous organ. I'll have these players
Play something like the murder of my father
Before mine uncle: I'll observe his looks;
I'll tent him to the quick: if he but blench,
I know my course. The spirit that I have seen
May be the devil; and the devil hath power
To assume a pleasing shape; yea, and perhaps
Out of my weakness and my melancholy,
As he is very potent with such spirits,
Abuses me to damn me. I'll have grounds
More relative than this. The play's the thing
Wherein I'll catch the conscience of the king.

[Exit.

Act III.

A room in the castle.
Enter King, Queen, Polonius, Ophelia, Rosencrantz,
and Guildenstern.

King. And can you, by no drift of circumstance,
 Get from him why he puts on this confusion,
 Grating so harshly all his days of quiet
 With turbulent and dangerous lunacy?
Rosencrantz. He does confess he feels himself distracted,
 But from what cause he will by no means speak.
Guildenstern. Nor do we find him forward to be sounded;
 But, with a crafty madness, keeps aloof,
 When we would bring him on to some confession
 Of his true state.
Queen. Did he receive you well?
Rosencrantz. Most like a gentleman.
Guildenstern. But with much forcing of his disposition.
Rosencrantz. Niggard of question, but of our demands
 Most free in his reply.
Queen. Did you assay him
 To any pastime?
Rosencrantz. Madam, it so fell out that certain players
 We o'er-raught on the way: of these we told him,
 And there did seem in him a kind of joy
 To hear of it: they are about the court,
 And, as I think, they have already order
 This night to play before him.

Polonius. 'Tis most true:
　　And he beseech'd me to entreat your majesties
　　To hear and see the matter.
King. With all my heart; and it doth much content me
　　To hear him so inclined.
　　Good gentlemen, give him a further edge,
　　And drive his purpose on to these delights.
Rosencrantz. We shall, my lord.

　　　　[*Exeunt Rosencrantz and Guildenstern.*

King. Sweet Gertrude, leave us too;
　　For we have closely sent for Hamlet hither,
　　That he, as 'twere by accident, may here
　　Affront Ophelia:
　　Her father and myself, lawful espials,
　　Will so bestow ourselves that, seeing unseen,
　　We may of their encounter frankly judge,
　　And gather by him, as he is behaved,
　　If 't be the affliction of his love or no
　　That thus he suffers Fortinbras.
Queen. I shall obey you:
　　And for your part, Ophelia, I do wish
　　That your good beauties be the happy cause
　　Of Hamlet's wildness: so shall I hope your virtues
　　Will bring him to his wonted way again,
　　To both your honours.
Ophelia. Madam, I wish it may.

　　　　　　　[*Exit Queen.*

Polonius. Ophelia, walk you here.
　　Gracious, so please you,
　　We will bestow ourselves.
　　[*To Ophelia*]
　　Read on this book;
　　That show of such an exercise may colour
　　Your loneliness. We are oft to blame in this, –
　　'Tis too much proved – that with devotion's visage
　　And pious action we do sugar o'er
　　The devil himself.

King. [*Aside*]
    O, 'tis too true!
    How smart a lash that speech doth give my conscience!
    The harlot's cheek, beautied with plastering art,
    Is not more ugly to the thing that helps it
    Than is my deed to my most painted word:
    O heavy burthen!
Polonius. I hear him coming: let's withdraw, my lord.

        [*Exeunt King and Polonius.*
          Enter Hamlet.

Hamlet. To be, or not to be: that is the question:
    Whether 'tis nobler in the mind to suffer
    The slings and arrows of outrageous fortune,
    Or to take arms against a sea of troubles,
    And by opposing end them? To die: to sleep;
    No more; and by a sleep to say we end
    The heart-ache, and the thousand natural shocks
    That flesh is heir to, 'tis a consummation
    Devoutly to be wish'd. To die, to sleep;
    To sleep: perchance to dream: ay, there's the rub;
    For in that sleep of death what dreams may come,
    When we have shuffled off this mortal coil,
    Must give us pause: there's the respect
    That makes calamity of so long life;
    For who would bear the whips and scorns of time,
    The oppressor's wrong, the proud man's contumely,
    The pangs of despised love, the law's delay,
    The insolence of office, and the spurns
    That patient merit of the unworthy takes,
    When he himself might his quietus make
    With a bare bodkin? who would fardels bear,
    To grunt and sweat under a weary life,
    But that the dread of something after death,
    The undiscover'd country from whose bourn
    No traveller returns, puzzles the will,
    And makes us rather bear those ills we have
    Than fly to others that we know not of?
    Thus conscience does make cowards of us all,
    And thus the native hue of resolution

Is sicklied o'er with the pale cast of thought,
And enterprises of great pitch and moment
With this regard their currents turn awry
And lose the name of action. Soft you now!
The fair Ophelia! Nymph, in thy orisons
Be all my sins remember'd.

Ophelia. Good my lord,
How does your honour for this many a day?

Hamlet. I humbly thank you: well, well, well.

Ophelia. My lord, I have remembrances of yours,
That I have longed long to re-deliver;
I pray you, now receive them.

Hamlet. No, not I;
I never gave you aught.

Ophelia. My honour'd lord, you know right well you did;
And with them words of so sweet breath composed
As made the things more rich: their perfume lost,
Take these again; for to the noble mind
Rich gifts wax poor when givers prove unkind.
There, my lord.

Hamlet. Ha, ha! are you honest?

Ophelia. My lord?

Hamlet. Are you fair?

Ophelia. What means your lordship?

Hamlet. That if you be honest and fair, your honesty
Should admit no discourse to your beauty.

Ophelia. Could beauty, my lord, have better commerce
Than with honesty?

Hamlet. Ay, truly; for the power of beauty will sooner
Transform honesty from what it is to a bawd than the
Force of honesty can translate beauty into his
Likeness: this was sometime a paradox, but now the
Time gives it proof. I did love you once.

Ophelia. Indeed, my lord, you made me believe so.

Hamlet. You should not have believed me; for virtue cannot
So inoculate our old stock but we shall relish of
It: I loved you not.

Ophelia. I was the more deceived.

Hamlet. Get thee to a nunnery: why wouldst thou be a
Breeder of sinners? I am myself indifferent honest;
But yet I could accuse me of such things that it

Were better my mother had not borne me: I am very
Proud, revengeful, ambitious; with more offences at
My beck than I have thoughts to put them in,
Imagination to give them shape, or time to act them
In. What should such fellows as I do crawling
Between heaven and earth? We are arrant knaves
All; believe none of us. Go thy ways to a nunnery.
Where's your father?

Ophelia. At home, my lord.

Hamlet. Let the doors be shut upon him, that he may play the
Fool no where but in's own house. Farewell.

Ophelia. O, help him, you sweet heavens!

Hamlet. If thou dost marry, I'll give thee this plague for
Thy dowry: be thou as chaste as ice, as pure as
Snow, thou shalt not escape calumny. Get thee to a
Nunnery, go: farewell. Or, if thou wilt needs
Marry, marry a fool; for wise men know well enough
What monsters you make of them. To a nunnery, go;
And quickly too. Farewell.

Ophelia. O heavenly powers, restore him!

Hamlet. I have heard of your paintings too, well enough; God
Hath given you one face, and you make yourselves
Another: you jig, you amble, and you lisp, and
Nick-name God's creatures, and make your wantonness
Your ignorance. Go to, I'll no more on't; it hath
Made me mad. I say, we will have no more marriages:
Those that are married already, all but one, shall
Live; the rest shall keep as they are. To a
Nunnery, go.

[*Exit.*

Ophelia. O, what a noble mind is here o'erthrown!
The courtier's, soldier's, scholar's, eye, tongue, sword:
The expectancy and rose of the fair state,
The glass of fashion and the mould of form,
The observed of all observers, quite, quite down!
And I, of ladies most deject and wretched,
That suck'd the honey of his music vows,
Now see that noble and most sovereign reason,
Like sweet bells jangled, out of tune and harsh;

That unmatch'd form and feature of blown youth
Blasted with ecstasy: O, woe is me,
To have seen what I have seen, see what I see!

Re-enter King *and* Polonius.

King. Love! his affections do not that way tend;
　　Nor what he spake, though it lack'd form a little,
　　Was not like madness. There's something in his soul
　　O'er which his melancholy sits on brood,
　　And I do doubt the hatch and the disclose
　　Will be some danger: which for to prevent,
　　I have in quick determination
　　Thus set it down: – he shall with speed to England,
　　For the demand of our neglected tribute:
　　Haply the seas and countries different
　　With variable objects shall expel
　　This something-settled matter in his heart,
　　Whereon his brains still beating puts him thus
　　From fashion of himself. What think you on 't?
Polonius. It shall do well: but yet do I believe
　　The origin and commencement of his grief
　　Sprung from neglected love. How now, Ophelia!
　　You need not tell us what Lord Hamlet said;
　　We heard it all. My lord, do as you please;
　　But, if you hold it fit, after the play,
　　Let his queen mother all alone entreat him
　　To show his grief: let her be round with him;
　　And I'll be placed, so please you, in the ear
　　Of all their conference. If she find him not,
　　To England send him, or confine him where
　　Your wisdom best shall think.
King. It shall be so:
　　Madness in great ones must not unwatch'd go.

[*Exeunt.*

SCENE TWO

A hall in the castle.
Enter Hamlet *and* Players.

Hamlet. Speak the speech, I pray you, as I pronounced it to
    You, trippingly on the tongue: but if you mouth it,
    As many of your players do, I had as lief the
    Town-crier spoke my lines. Nor do not saw the air
    Too much with your hand, thus; but use all gently:
    For in the very torrent, tempest, and, as I may say,
    Whirlwind of your passion, you must acquire and beget
    A temperance that may give it smoothness. O, it
    Offends me to the soul to hear a robustious
    Periwig-pated fellow tear a passion to tatters, to
    Very rags, to split the ears of the groundlings, who,
    For the most part, are capable of nothing but
    Inexplicable dumb-shows and noise: I would have such
    A fellow whipped for o'er-doing Termagant; it
    Out-herods Herod: pray you, avoid it.
First Play. I warrant your honour.
Hamlet. Be not too tame neither, but let your own discretion
    Be your tutor: suit the action to the word, the
    Word to the action; with this special observance,
    That you o'er-step not the modesty of nature: for
    Any thing so overdone is from the purpose of playing,
    Whose end, both at the first and now, was and is, to
    Hold, as 'twere, the mirror up to nature; to show
    Virtue her own feature, scorn her own image, and the very
    Age and body of the time his form and pressure. Now

This overdone or come tardy off, though it make the
Unskilful laugh, cannot but make the judicious grieve; the
Censure of the which one must in your allowance
O'erweigh a whole theatre of others. O, there be
Players that I have seen play, and heard others
Praise, and that highly, not to speak it profanely,
That neither having the accent of Christians nor
The gait of Christian, pagan, nor man, have so
Strutted and bellowed, that I have thought some of
Nature's journeymen had made men, and not made them
Well, they imitated humanity so abominably.
First Play. I hope we have reformed that indifferently with us,
Sir.
Hamlet. O, reform it altogether. And let those that play
Your clowns speak no more than is set down for them:
For there be of them that will themselves laugh, to
Set on some quantity of barren spectators to laugh
Too, though in the mean time some necessary
Question of the play be then to be considered:
That's villanous, and shows a most pitiful ambition
In the fool that uses it. Go, make you ready.

[*Exeunt Players.*
Enter Polonius, Rosencrantz, *and* Guildenstern.

How now, my lord! will the king hear this piece of work?
Polonius. And the queen too, and that presently.
Hamlet. Bid the players make haste.

[*Exit Polonius.*]

Will you two help to hasten them?
Rosencrantz. Guildenstern. We will, my lord.

[*Exeunt Rosencrantz and Guildenstern.*

Hamlet. What ho! Horatio!
Enter Horatio.
Horatio. Here, sweet lord, at your service.
Hamlet. Horatio, thou art e'en as just a man
As e'er my conversation coped withal.

Horatio. O, my dear lord, –
Hamlet. Nay, do not think I flatter;
 For what advancement may I hope from thee,
 That no revenue hast but thy good spirits,
 To feed and clothe thee? Why should the poor be flatter'd?
 No, let the candied tongue lick absurd pomp,
 And crook the pregnant hinges of the knee
 Where thrift may follow fawning. Dost thou hear?
 Since my dear soul was mistress of her choice,
 And could of men distinguish, her election
 Hath seal'd thee for herself: for thou hast been
 As one, in suffering all, that suffers nothing;
 A man that fortune's buffets and rewards
 Hast ta'en with equal thanks: and blest are those
 Whose blood and judgement are so well commingled
 That they are not a pipe for fortune's finger
 To sound what stop she please. Give me that man
 That is not passion's slave, and I will wear him
 In my heart's core, ay, in my heart of heart,
 As I do thee. Something too much of this.
 There is a play to-night before the king;
 One scene of it comes near the circumstance
 Which I have told thee of my father's death:
 I prithee, when thou seest that act a-foot,
 Even with the very comment of thy soul
 Observe my uncle: if his occulted guilt
 Do not itself unkennel in one speech,
 It is a damned ghost that we have seen,
 And my imaginations are as foul
 As Vulcan's stithy. Give him heedful note;
 For I mine eyes will rivet to his face,
 And after we will both our judgements join
 In censure of his seeming.
Horatio. Well, my lord:
 If he steal aught the whilst this play is playing,
 And 'scape detecting, I will pay the theft.
Hamlet. They are coming to the play:
 I must be idle:
 Get you a place.

Danish march. A flourish. Enter King, Queen, Polonius,
Ophelia, Rosencrantz, Guildenstern, *and other Lords attendant,
with the Guard carrying torches.*

King. How fares our cousin Hamlet?
Hamlet. Excellent, i' faith; of the chameleon's dish: I eat
    The air, promise-crammed: you cannot feed capons so.
King. I have nothing with this answer, Hamlet; these words
    Are not mine.
Hamlet. No, nor mine now.
    [*To Polonius*]
    My lord, you played once i' the university, you Say?
Polonius. That did I, my lord, and was accounted a good actor.
Hamlet. What did you enact?
Polonius. I did enact Julius Cæsar: I was killed i' the
    Capitol; Brutus killed me.
Hamlet. It was a brute part of him to kill so capital a calf
    There. Be the players ready?
Rosencrantz. Ay, my lord; they stay upon your patience.
Queen. Come hither, my dear Hamlet, sit by me.
Hamlet. No, good mother, here's metal more attractive.
Polonius. [*To the King*]
    O, ho! do you mark that?
Hamlet. Lady, shall I lie in your lap?

[*Lying down at Ophelia's feet.*

Ophelia. No, my lord.
Hamlet. I mean, my head upon your lap?
Ophelia. Ay, my lord.
Hamlet. Do you think I meant country matters?
Ophelia. I think nothing, my lord.
Hamlet. That's a fair thought to lie between maids' legs.
Ophelia. What is, my lord?
Hamlet. Nothing.
Ophelia. You are merry, my lord.
Hamlet. Who, I?
Ophelia. Ay, my lord.
Hamlet. O God, your only jig-maker. What should a man do
    But be merry? for, look you, how cheerfully my
    Mother looks, and my father died within 's two hours.

Ophelia. Nay, 'tis twice two months, my lord.
Hamlet. So long? Nay, then, let the devil wear black, for
    I'll have a suit of sables. O heavens! die two
    Months ago, and not forgotten yet? Then there's
    Hope a great man's memory may outlive his life half
    A year: but, by'r lady, he must build churches
    Then; or else shall he suffer not thinking on, with
    The hobby-horse, whose epitaph is, 'For, O, for, O,
    The hobby-horse is forgot.'

    Hautboys play. The dumb-show enters.
    Enter a King *and a* Queen *very lovingly; the* Queen *embracing him, and he her. She kneels, and makes show of protestation unto him. He takes her up, and declines his head upon her neck: lays him down upon a bank of flowers: she, seeing him asleep, leaves him. Anon comes in a fellow, takes off his crown, kisses it, and pours poison in the* King's *ears, and exit. The* Queen *returns; finds the* King *dead, and makes passionate action. The* Poisoner, *with some two or three* Mutes, *comes in again, seeming to lament with her. The dead body is carried away. The* Poisoner *wooes the* Queen *with gifts: she seems loath and unwilling awhile, but in the end accepts his love.*
    [Exeunt.

Ophelia. What means this, my lord?
Hamlet. Marry, this is miching mallecho; it means mischief.
Ophelia. Belike this show imports the argument of the play.
Enter Prologue.
Hamlet. We shall know by this fellow: the players cannot
    Keep counsel; they'll tell all.
Ophelia. Will he tell us what this show meant?
Hamlet. Ay, or any show that you'll show him: be not you
    Ashamed to show, he'll not shame to tell you what it means.
Ophelia. You are naught, you are naught: I'll mark the play.
Prologue. For us, and for our tragedy,
    Here stooping to your clemency,
    We beg your hearing patiently.
Hamlet. Is this a prologue, or the posy of a ring?
Ophelia. 'tis brief, my lord.
      Hamlet. As woman's love.

Enter two Players, King *and* Queen.

P. King. Full thirty times hath Phœbus' cart gone round
    Neptune's salt wash and Tellus' orbed ground,
    And thirty dozen moons with borrowed sheen
    About the world have times twelve thirties been,
    Since love our hearts and Hymen did our hands
    Unite commutual in most sacred bands.
P. Queen. So many journeys may the sun and moon
    Make us again count o'er ere love be done!
    But, woe is me, you are so sick of late,
    So far from cheer and from your former state,
    That I distrust you. Yet, though I distrust,
    Discomfort you, my lord, it nothing must:
    For women's fear and love holds quantity,
    In neither aught, or in extremity.
    Now, what my love is, proof hath made you know,
    And as my love is sized, my fear is so:
    Where love is great, the littlest doubts are fear,
    Where little fears grow great, great love grows there.
P. King. Faith, I must leave thee, love, and shortly too;
    My operant powers their functions leave to do:
    And thou shalt live in this fair world behind,
    Honour'd, beloved; and haply one as kind
    For husband shalt thou –
P. Queen. O, confound the rest!
    Such love must needs be treason in my breast:
    In second husband let me be accurst!
    None wed the second but who kill'd the first.
Hamlet. [*Aside*] Wormwood, wormwood.
P. Queen. The instances that second marriage move
    Are base respects of thrift, but none of love:
    A second time I kill my husband dead,
    When second husband kisses me in bed.
P. King. I do believe you think what now you speak,
    But what we do determine oft we break.
    Purpose is but the slave to memory,
    Of violent birth but poor validity:
    Which now, like fruit unripe, sticks on the tree,
    But fall unshaken when they mellow be.
    Most necessary 'tis that we forget

To pay ourselves what to ourselves is debt:
What to ourselves in passion we propose,
The passion ending, doth the purpose lose.
The violence of either grief or joy
Their own enactures with themselves destroy:
Where joy most revels, grief doth most lament;
Grief joys, joy grieves, on slender accident.
This world is not for aye, nor 'tis not strange
That even our loves should with our fortunes change,
For 'tis a question left us yet to prove,
Whether love lead fortune or else fortune love.
The great man down, you mark his favourite flies;
The poor advanced makes friends of enemies:
And hitherto doth love on fortune tend;
For who not needs shall never lack a friend,
And who in want a hollow friend doth try
Directly seasons him his enemy.
But, orderly to end where I begun,
Our wills and fates do so contrary run,
That our devices still are overthrown,
Our thoughts are ours, their ends none of our own:
So think thou wilt no second husband wed,
But die thy thoughts when thy first lord is dead.

P. Queen. Nor earth to me give food nor heaven light!
Sport and repose lock from me day and night!
To desperation turn my trust and hope!
An anchor's cheer in prison be my scope!
Each opposite, that blanks the face of joy,
Meet what I would have well and it destroy!
Both here and hence pursue me lasting strife,
If, once a widow, ever I be wife!

Hamlet. If she should break it now!

P. King. 'Tis deeply sworn. Sweet, leave me here awhile;
My spirits grow dull, and fain I would beguile
The tedious day with sleep. [*Sleeps.*

P. Queen. Sleep rock thy brain;
And never come mischance between us twain! [*Exit.*

Hamlet. Madam, how like you this play?

Queen. The lady doth protest too much, methinks.

Hamlet. O, but she'll keep her word.

King. Have you heard the argument? Is there no offence in't?

Hamlet. No, no, they do but jest, poison in jest; no offence
I' the world.
King. What do you call the play?
Hamlet. The Mouse-trap. Marry, how? Tropically. This play
Is the image of a murder done in Vienna: Gonzago is
The duke's name; his wife, Baptista: you shall see
Anon; 'tis a knavish piece of work: but what o'
That? your majesty, and we that have free souls, it
Touches us not: let the galled jade wince, our
Withers are unwrung.

Enter Lucianus. This is one Lucianus, nephew to the king.

Ophelia. You are as good as a chorus, my lord.
Hamlet. I could interpret between you and your love, if I
Could see the puppets dallying.
Ophelia. You are keen, my lord, you are keen.
Hamlet. It would cost you a groaning to take off my edge.
Ophelia. Still better, and worse.
Hamlet. So you must take your husbands. Begin, murderer;
Pox, leave thy damnable faces, and begin. Come:
The croaking raven doth bellow for revenge.
Lucianus. Thoughts black, hands apt, drugs fit, and time agreeing;
Confederate season, else no creature seeing;
Thou mixture rank, of midnight weeds collected,
With Hecate's ban thrice blasted, thrice infected,
Thy natural magic and dire property,
On wholesome life usurp immediately.

[*Pours the poison into the sleeper's ear.*

Hamlet. He poisons him i' the garden for his estate. His
Name's Gonzago: the story is extant, and written in very
Choice Italian: you shall see anon how the murderer
Gets the love of Gonzago's wife.
Ophelia. The king rises.
Hamlet. What, frighted with false fire!
Queen. How fares my lord?
Polonius. Give o'er the play.
King. Give me some light. Away!
Polonius. Lights, lights, lights!

[Exeunt all but Hamlet and Horatio.

Hamlet. Why, let the stricken deer go weep,
    The hart ungalled play;
    For some must watch, while some must sleep:
    Thus runs the world away.
    Would not this, sir, and a forest of feathers – if
    The rest of my fortunes turn Turk with me – with two
    Provincial roses on my razed shoes, get me a
    Fellowship in a cry of players, sir?
Horatio. Half a share.
Hamlet. A whole one, I. For thou dost know, O Damon dear,
    This realm dismantled was
    Of Jove himself; and now reigns here
    A very, very – pajock.
Horatio. You might have rhymed.
Hamlet. O good Horatio, I'll take the ghost's word for a
    Thousand pound. Didst perceive?
Horatio. Very well, my lord.
Hamlet. Upon the talk of the poisoning?
Horatio. I did very well note him.
Hamlet. Ah, ha! Come, some music! come, the recorders!
    For if the king like not the comedy,
    Why then, belike, he likes it not, perdy.
    Come, some music!

Re-enter Rosencrantz *and* Guildenstern.

Guildenstern. Good my lord, vouchsafe me a word with you.
Hamlet. Sir, a whole history.
Guildenstern. The king, sir, –
Hamlet. Ay, sir, what of him?
Guildenstern. Is in his retirement marvellous distempered.
Hamlet. With drink, sir?
Guildenstern. No, my lord, rather with choler.
Hamlet. Your wisdom should show itself more richer to
    Signify this to the doctor; for, for me to put him
    To his purgation would perhaps plunge him into far
    More choler.
Guildenstern. Good my lord, put your discourse into some frame, and
    Start not so wildly from my affair.

Hamlet. I am tame, sir: pronounce.

Guildenstern. The queen, your mother, in most great affliction of
    Spirit, hath sent me to you.

Hamlet. You are welcome.

Guildenstern. Nay, good my lord, this courtesy is not of the right
    Breed. If it shall please you to make me a
    Wholesome answer, I will do your mother's
    Commandment: if not, your pardon and my return
    Shall be the end of my business.

Hamlet. Sir, I cannot.

Guildenstern. What, my lord?

Hamlet. Make you a wholesome answer; my wit's diseased: but,
    Sir, such answer as I can make, you shall command;
    Or rather, as you say, my mother: therefore no
    More, but to the matter: my mother, you say, –

Rosencrantz. Then thus she says; your behaviour hath struck her
    Into amazement and admiration.

Hamlet. O wonderful son, that can so astonish a mother! But
    Is there no sequel at the heels of this mother's
    Admiration? Impart.

Rosencrantz. She desires to speak with you in her closet, ere you
    Go to bed.

Hamlet. We shall obey, were she ten times our mother. Have
    You any further trade with us?

Rosencrantz. My lord, you once did love me.

Hamlet. So I do still, by these pickers and stealers.

Rosencrantz. Good my lord, what is your cause of distemper? you
    Do surely bar the door upon your own liberty, if
    You deny your griefs to your friend.

Hamlet. Sir, I lack advancement.

Rosencrantz. How can that be, when you have the voice of the king
    Himself for your succession in Denmark?

Hamlet. Ay, sir, but 'while the grass grows,' – the proverb
    Is something musty.

Re-enter Players *with recorders.*

O, the recorders! let me see one. To withdraw with
You: – why do you go about to recover the wind of me,
As if you would drive me into a toil?

Guildenstern. O, my lord, if my duty be too bold, my love is too
    Unmannerly.
Hamlet. I do not well understand that. Will you play upon
    This pipe?
Guildenstern. My lord, I cannot.
Hamlet. I pray you.
Guildenstern. Believe me, I cannot.
Hamlet. I do beseech you.
Guildenstern. I know no touch of it, my lord.
Hamlet. It is as easy as lying: govern these ventages with
    Your fingers and thumb, give it breath with your
    Mouth, and it will discourse most eloquent music.
    Look you, these are the stops.
Guildenstern. But these cannot I command to any utterance of
    Harmony; I have not the skill.
Hamlet. Why, look you now, how unworthy a thing you make of
    Me! You would play upon me; you would seem to know
    My stops; you would pluck out the heart of my
    Mystery; you would sound me from my lowest note to
    The top of my compass: and there is much music,
    Excellent voice, in this little organ; yet cannot
    You make it speak. 'Sblood, do you think I am
    Easier to be played on than a pipe? Call me what
    Instrument you will, though you can fret me, yet you
    Cannot play upon me.

Enter Polonius.

God bless you, sir!
Polonius. My lord, the queen would speak with you, and
    Presently.
Hamlet. Do you see yonder cloud that's almost in shape of A camel?
Polonius. By the mass, and 'tis like a camel, indeed.
Hamlet. Methinks it is like a weasel.
Polonius. It is backed like a weasel.
Hamlet. Or like a whale?
Polonius. Very like a whale.
Hamlet. Then I will come to my mother by and by. They fool
    Me to the top of my bent. I will come by and by.
Polonius. I will say so.

[*Exit Polonius.*

Hamlet. 'By and by' is easily said. Leave me, friends.

[*Exeunt all but Hamlet.*

'Tis now the very witching time of night,
    When churchyards yawn, and hell itself breathes out
    Contagion to this world: now could I drink hot blood,
    And do such bitter business as the day
    Would quake to look on. Soft! now to my mother.
    O heart, lose not thy nature; let not ever
    The soul of Nero enter this firm bosom:
    Let me be cruel, not unnatural:
    I will speak daggers to her, but use none;
    My tongue and soul in this be hypocrites;
    How in my words soever she be shent,
    To give them seals never, my soul, consent!

[*Exit.*

SCENE THREE

A room in the castle.
Enter King, Rosencrantz, *and* Guildenstern.

King. I like him not, nor stands it safe with us
    To let his madness range. Therefore prepare you;
    I your commission will forthwith dispatch,
    And he to England shall along with you:
    The terms of our estate may not endure
    Hazard so near us as doth hourly grow
    Out of his lunacies.
Guildenstern. We will ourselves provide:
    Most holy and religious fear it is
    To keep those many many bodies safe
    That live and feed upon your majesty.
Rosencrantz. The single and peculiar life is bound
    With all the strength and armour of the mind
    To keep itself from noyance; but much more
    That spirit upon whose weal depends and rests
    The lives of many. The cease of majesty
    Dies not alone, but like a gulf doth draw
    What's near it with it: it is a massy wheel,
    Fix'd on the summit of the highest mount,
    To whose huge spokes ten thousand lesser things
    Are mortised and adjoin'd; which, when it falls,
    Each small annexment, petty consequence,
    Attends the boisterous ruin. Never alone
    Did the king sigh, but with a general groan.
King. Arm you, I pray you, to this speedy voyage,
    For we will fetters put about this fear,
    Which now goes too free-footed.
Rosencrantz. We will haste us. *Guildenstern.*

[*Exeunt Rosencrantz and Guildenstern.*
Enter Polonius.

Polonius. My lord, he's going to his mother's closet:
　Behind the arras I'll convey myself,
　To hear the process; I'll warrant she'll tax him home:
　And, as you said, and wisely was it said,
　'Tis meet that some more audience than a mother,
　Since nature makes them partial, should o'erhear
　The speech, of vantage. Fare you well, my liege:
　I'll call upon you ere you go to bed,
　And tell you what I know.
King. Thanks, dear my lord.

[*Exit Polonius.*

O, my offence is rank, it smells to heaven;
It hath the primal eldest curse upon't,
A brother's murder. Pray can I not,
Though inclination be as sharp as will:
My stronger guilt defeats my strong intent,
And like a man to double business bound,
I stand in pause where I shall first begin,
And both neglect. What if this cursed hand
Were thicker than itself with brother's blood,
Is there not rain enough in the sweet heavens
To wash it white as snow? Whereto serves mercy
But to confront the visage of offence?
And what's in prayer but this twofold force,
To be forestalled ere we come to fall,
Or pardon'd being down? Then I'll look up;
My fault is past. But O, what form of prayer
Can serve my turn? 'Forgive me my foul murder?'
That cannot be, since I am still possess'd
Of those effects for which I did the murder,
My crown, mine own ambition and my queen.
May one be pardon'd and retain the offence?
In the corrupted currents of this world
Offence's gilded hand may shove by justice,
And oft 'tis seen the wicked prize itself
Buys out the law: but 'tis not so above;

There is no shuffling, there the action lies
In his true nature, and we ourselves compell'd
Even to the teeth and forehead of our faults
To give in evidence. What then? what rests?
Try what repentance can: what can it not?
Yet what can it when one can not repent?
O wretched state! O bosom black as death!
O limed soul, that struggling to be free
Art more engaged! Help, angels! make assay!
Bow, stubborn knees, and, heart with strings of steel,
Be soft as sinews of the new-born babe!
All may be well. [*Retires and kneels.*

Enter Hamlet.

Hamlet. Now might I do it pat, now he is praying;
    And now I'll do't: and so he goes to heaven:
    And so am I revenged. That would be scann'd:
    A villain kills my father; and for that,
    I, his sole son, do this same villain send
    To heaven. O, this is hire and salary, not revenge.
    He took my father grossly, full of bread,
    With all his crimes broad blown, as flush as May;
    And how his audit stands who knows save heaven?
    But in our circumstance and course of thought,
    'Tis heavy with him: and am I then revenged,
    To take him in the purging of his soul,
    When he is fit and season'd for his passage?
    No. Up, sword, and know thou a more horrid hent:
    When he is drunk asleep, or in his rage,
    Or in the incestuous pleasure of his bed;
    At game, a-swearing, or about some act
    That has no relish of salvation in 't;
    Then trip him, that his heels may kick at heaven
    And that his soul may be as damn'd and black
    As hell, whereto it goes. My mother stays:
    This physic but prolongs thy sickly days. [*Exit.*
King. [*Rising*] My words fly up, my thoughts remain below:
    Words without thoughts never to heaven go.

[*Exit.*

SCENE FOUR

The Queen's closet.
Enter Queen *and* Polonius.

Polonius. He will come straight. Look you lay home to him:
    Tell him his pranks have been too broad to bear with,
    And that your grace hath screen'd and stood between
    Much heat and him. I'll sconce me even here.
    Pray you, be round with him.
Hamlet. [*Within*
    Mother, mother, mother!
Queen. I'll warrant you; fear me not.
    Withdraw, I hear him coming.
[*Polonius hides behind the arras.*
Enter Hamlet.
Hamlet. Now, mother, what's the matter?
Queen. Hamlet, thou hast thy father much offended.
Hamlet. Mother, you have my father much offended.
Queen. Come, come, you answer with an idle tongue.
Hamlet. Go, go, you question with a wicked tongue.
Queen. Why, how now, Hamlet!
Hamlet. What's the matter now?
Queen. Have you forgot me?
Hamlet. No, by the rood, not so:
    You are the queen, your husband's brother's wife;
    And – would it were not so! – you are my mother.
Queen. Nay, then, I'll set those to you that can speak.
Hamlet. Come, come, and sit you down; you shall not budge;
    You go not till I set you up a glass
    Where you may see the inmost part of you.

Queen. What wilt thou do? thou wilt not murder me?
　　Help, help, ho!
Polonius. [*Behind*] What, ho! help, help, help!
Hamlet. [*Drawing*] How now! a rat? Dead, for a ducat, dead!
[*Makes a pass through the arras.*
Polonius. [*Behind*] O, I am slain!

[*Falls and dies.*

Queen. O me, what hast thou done?
Hamlet. Nay, I know not: is it the king?
Queen. O, what a rash and bloody deed is this!
Hamlet. A bloody deed! almost as bad, good mother,
　　As kill a king, and marry with his brother.
Queen. As kill a king!
Hamlet. Ay, lady, 'twas my word.

[*Lifts up the arras and discovers Polonius.*

　　Thou wretched, rash, intruding fool, farewell!
　　I took thee for thy better: take thy fortune;
　　Thou find'st to be too busy is some danger.
　　Leave wringing of your hands: peace! sit you down,
　　And let me wring your heart: for so I shall,
　　If it be made of penetrable stuff;
　　If damned custom have not brass'd it so,
　　That it be proof and bulwark against sense.
Queen. What have I done, that thou darest wag thy tongue
　　In noise so rude against me?
Hamlet. Such an act
　　That blurs the grace and blush of modesty,
　　Calls virtue hypocrite, takes off the rose
　　From the fair forehead of an innocent love,
　　And sets a blister there; makes marriage vows
　　As false as dicers' oaths: O, such a deed
　　As from the body of contraction plucks
　　The very soul, and sweet religion makes
　　A rhapsody of words: heaven's face doth glow;
　　Yea, this solidity and compound mass,
　　With tristful visage, as against the doom,
　　Is thought-sick at the act.

Queen. Ay me, what act,
    That roars so loud and thunders in the index?
Hamlet. Look here, upon this picture, and on this,
    The counterfeit presentment of two brothers.
    See what a grace was seated on this brow;
    Hyperion's curls, the front of Jove himself,
    An eye like Mars, to threaten and command;
    A station like the herald Mercury
    New-lighted on a heaven-kissing hill;
    A combination and a form indeed,
    Where every god did seem to set his seal
    To give the world assurance of a man:
    This was your husband. Look you now, what follows:
    Here is your husband; like a mildew'd ear,
    Blasting his wholesome brother. Have you eyes?
    Could you on this fair mountain leave to feed,
    And batten on this moor? Ha! have you eyes?
    You cannot call it love, for at your age
    The hey-day in the blood is tame, it's humble,
    And waits upon the judgement: and what judgement
    Would step from this to this? Sense sure you have,
    Else could you not have motion: but sure that sense
    Is apoplex'd: for madness would not err,
    Nor sense to ecstasy was ne'er so thrall'd
    But it reserved some quantity of choice,
    To serve in such a difference. What devil was't
    That thus hath cozen'd you at hoodman-blind?
    Eyes without feeling, feeling without sight,
    Ears without hands or eyes, smelling sans all,
    Or but a sickly part of one true sense
    Could not so mope.
    O shame! where is thy blush? Rebellious hell,
    If thou canst mutine in a matron's bones,
    To flaming youth let virtue be as wax
    And melt in her own fire: proclaim no shame
    When the compulsive ardour gives the charge,
    Since frost itself as actively doth burn,
    And reason panders will.
Queen. O Hamlet, speak no more:
    Thou turn'st mine eyes into my very soul,
    And there I see such black and grained spots

As will not leave their tinct.

Hamlet. Nay, but to live In the rank sweat of an enseamed bed,
Stew'd in corruption, honeying and making love
Over the nasty sty, –

Queen. O, speak to me no more;
These words like daggers enter in my ears;
No more, sweet Hamlet!

Hamlet. A murderer and a villain;
A slave that is not twentieth part the tithe
Of your precedent lord; a vice of kings;
A cutpurse of the empire and the rule,
That from a shelf the precious diadem stole
And put it in his pocket!

Queen. No more!

Hamlet. A king of shreds and patches –

Enter Ghost.

Save me, and hover o'er me with your wings,
You heavenly guards!
What would your gracious figure?

Queen. Alas, he's mad!

Hamlet. Do you not come your tardy son to chide,
That, lapsed in time and passion, lets go by
The important acting of your dread command?
O, say!

Ghost. Do not forget: this visitation
Is but to whet thy almost blunted purpose.
But look, amazement on thy mother sits:
O, step between her and her fighting soul:
Conceit in weakest bodies strongest works:
Speak to her, Hamlet.

Hamlet. How is it with you, lady?

Queen. Alas, how is't with you,
That you do bend your eye on vacancy
And with the incorporal air do hold discourse?
Forth at your eyes your spirits wildly peep;
And, as the sleeping soldiers in the alarm,
Your bedded hairs, like life in excrements,
Start up and stand an end. O gentle son,
Upon the heat and flame of thy distemper

Sprinkle cool patience. Whereon do you look?
Hamlet. On him, on him!
  Look you, how pale he glares!
  His form and cause conjoin'd, preaching to stones,
  Would make them capable. Do not look upon me,
  Lest with this piteous action you convert
  My stern effects: then what I have to do
  Will want true colour; tears perchance for blood.
Queen. To whom do you speak this?
Hamlet. Do you see nothing there?
Queen. Nothing at all; yet all that is I see.
Hamlet. Nor did you nothing hear?
Queen. No, nothing but ourselves.
Hamlet. Why, look you there! look, how it steals away!
  My father, in his habit as he lived!
  Look, where he goes, even now, out at the portal!

      [*Exit Ghost.*

Queen. This is the very coinage of your brain:
  This bodiless creation ecstasy
  Is very cunning in.
Hamlet. Ecstasy!
  My pulse, as yours, doth temperately keep time,
  And makes as healthful music: it is not madness
  That I have utter'd: bring me to the test,
  And I the matter will re-word, which madness
  Would gambol from. Mother, for love of grace,
  Lay not that flattering unction to your soul,
  That not your trespass but my madness speaks:
  It will but skin and film the ulcerous place,
  Whiles rank corruption, mining all within,
  Infects unseen. Confess yourself to heaven;
  Repent what's past, avoid what is to come,
  And do not spread the compost on the weeds,
  To make them ranker. Forgive me this my virtue,
  For in the fatness of these pursy times
  Virtue itself of vice must pardon beg,
  Yea, curb and woo for leave to do him good.
Queen. O Hamlet, thou hast cleft my heart in twain.
Hamlet. O, throw away the worser part of it,

And live the purer with the other half.
Good night: but go not to my uncle's bed;
Assume a virtue, if you have it not.
That monster, custom, who all sense doth eat,
Of habits devil, is angel yet in this,
That to the use of actions fair and good
He likewise gives a frock or livery,
That aptly is put on. Refrain to-night,
And that shall lend a kind of easiness
To the next abstinence; the next more easy;
For use almost can change the stamp of nature,
And either ... the devil, or throw him out
With wondrous potency. Once more, good night:
And when you are desirous to be blest,
I'll blessing beg of you. For this same lord,

[*Pointing to Polonius.*

I do repent: but heaven hath pleased it so,
To punish me with this, and this with me,
That I must be their scourge and minister.
I will bestow him, and will answer well
The death I gave him. So, again, good night.
I must be cruel, only to be kind:
Thus bad begins, and worse remains behind.
One word more, good lady.
Queen. What shall I do?
Hamlet. Not this, by no means, that I bid you do:
Let the bloat king tempt you again to bed;
Pinch wanton on your cheek, call you his mouse;
And let him, for a pair of reechy kisses,
Or paddling in your neck with his damn'd fingers,
Make you to ravel all this matter out,
That I essentially am not in madness,
But mad in craft. 'Twere good you let him know;
For who, that's but a queen, fair, sober, wise,
Would from a paddock, from a bat, a gib,
Such dear concernings hide? who would do so?
No, in despite of sense and secrecy,
Unpeg the basket on the house's top,
Let the birds fly, and like the famous ape,

To try conclusions, in the basket creep
And break your own neck down.
Queen. Be thou assured, if words be made of breath
And breath of life, I have no life to breathe
What thou hast said to me.
Hamlet. I must to England; you know that?
Queen. Alack, I had forgot: 'tis so concluded on.
Hamlet. There's letters seal'd: and my two schoolfellows,
Whom I will trust as I will adders fang'd,
They bear the mandate; they must sweep my way,
And marshal me to knavery. Let it work;
For 'tis the sport to have the enginer
Hoist with his own petar: and't shall go hard
But I will delve one yard below their mines,
And blow them at the moon: O, 'tis most sweet
When in one line two crafts directly meet.
This man shall set me packing:
I'll lug the guts into the neighbour room.
Mother, good night. Indeed this counsellor
Is now most still, most secret and most grave,
Who was in life a foolish prating knave.
Come, sir, to draw toward an end with you.
Good night, mother.

[*Exeunt severally; Hamlet dragging in Polonius.*]

Act IV.

SCENE ONE

A room in the castle.
Enter King, Queen, Rosencrantz, *and* Guildenstern.

King. There's matter in these sighs, these profound heaves:
You must translate: 'tis fit we understand them.
Where is your son?
Queen. Bestow this place on us a little while.

[*Exeunt Rosencrantz and Guildenstern.*

Ah, mine own lord, what have I seen to-night!
King. What, Gertrude? How does Hamlet?
Queen. Mad as the sea and wind, when both contend
Which is the mightier: in his lawless fit,
Behind the arras hearing something stir,
Whips out his rapier, cries 'a rat, a rat!'
And in this brainish apprehension kills
The unseen good old man.
King. O heavy deed!
It had been so with us, had we been there:
His liberty is full of threats to all,
To you yourself, to us, to every one.
Alas, how shall this bloody deed be answer'd?
It will be laid to us, whose providence
Should have kept short, restrain'd and out of haunt,
This mad young man: but so much was our love,
We would not understand what was most fit,

But, like the owner of a foul disease,
To keep it from divulging, let it feed
Even on the pith of life. Where is he gone?
Queen. To draw apart the body he hath kill'd:
O'er whom his very madness, like some ore
Among a mineral of metals base,
Shows itself pure; he weeps for what is done.
King. O Gertrude, come away!
The sun no sooner shall the mountains touch,
But we will ship him hence: and this vile deed
We must, with all our majesty and skill,
Both countenance and excuse. Ho, Guildenstern!

Re-enter Rosencrantz *and* Guildenstern.

Friends both, go join you with some further aid:
Hamlet in madness hath Polonius slain,
And from his mother's closet hath he dragg'd him:
Go seek him out; speak fair, and bring the body
Into the chapel. I pray you, haste in this.

[*Exeunt Rosencrantz and Guildenstern.*

Come, Gertrude, we'll call up our wisest friends;
And let them know, both what we mean to do,
And what's untimely done....
Whose whisper o'er the world's diameter
As level as the cannon to his blank
Transports his poison'd shot, may miss our name
And hit the woundless air. O, come away!
My soul is full of discord and dismay.

[*Exeunt.*

SCENE TWO

Another room in the castle.
Enter Hamlet.

Hamlet. Safely stowed.
Rosencrantz. [*Within*Hamlet! Lord Hamlet! *Guildenstern.*
Hamlet. But soft, what noise? who calls on Hamlet?
    O, here they come.
Enter Rosencrantz *and* Guildenstern.
Rosencrantz. What have you done, my lord, with the dead body?
Hamlet. Compounded it with dust, whereto 'tis kin.
Rosencrantz. Tell us where 'tis, that we may take it thence
    And bear it to the chapel.
Hamlet. Do not believe it.
Rosencrantz. Believe what?
Hamlet. That I can keep your counsel and not mine own.
    Besides, to be demanded of a sponge! what
    Replication should be made by the son of a king?
Rosencrantz. Take you me for a sponge, my lord?
Hamlet. Ay, sir; that soaks up the king's countenance, his
    Rewards, his authorities. But such officers do the
    King best service in the end: he keeps them, like
    An ape, in the corner of his jaw; first mouthed, to
    Be last swallowed: when he needs what you have
    Gleaned, it is but squeezing you, and, sponge, you
    Shall be dry again.
Rosencrantz. I understand you not, my lord.
Hamlet. I am glad of it: a knavish speech sleeps in a
    Foolish ear.

Rosencrantz. My lord, you must tell us where the body is, and go
    With us to the king.
Hamlet. The body is with the king, but the king is not with
    The body. The king is a thing –
Guildenstern. A thing, my lord?
Hamlet. Of nothing: bring me to him. Hide fox, and all after.

[*Exeunt.*

SCENE THREE

Another room in the castle.
Enter King, *attended.*

King. I have sent to seek him, and to find the body.
  How dangerous is it that this man goes loose!
  Yet must not we put the strong law on him:
  He's loved of the distracted multitude,
  Who like not in their judgement, but their eyes;
  And where 'tis so, the offender's scourge is weigh'd,
  But never the offence. To bear all smooth and even,
  This sudden sending him away must seem
  Deliberate pause: diseases desperate grown
  By desperate appliance are relieved,
  Or not at all.
Enter Rosencrantz.
  How now! what hath befall'n?
Rosencrantz. Where the dead body is bestow'd, my lord,
  We cannot get from him.
King. But where is he?
Rosencrantz. Without, my lord; guarded, to know your pleasure.
King. Bring him before us.
Rosencrantz. Ho, Guildenstern! bring in my lord.
Enter Hamlet *and* Guildenstern.
King. Now, Hamlet, where's Polonius?
Hamlet. At supper.
King. At supper! where?
Hamlet. Not where he eats, but where he is eaten: a certain
  convocation of politic worms are e'en at him. Your
  worm is your only emperor for diet: we fat all

creatures else to fat us, and we fat ourselves for
maggots: your fat king and your lean beggar is but
variable service, two dishes, but to one table:
that's the end.

King. Alas, alas!

Hamlet. A man may fish with the worm that hath eat of a
king, and eat of the fish that hath fed of that worm.

King. What dost thou mean by this?

Hamlet. Nothing but to show you how a king may go a
progress through the guts of a beggar.

King. Where is Polonius?

Hamlet. In heaven; send thither to see: if your messenger
find him not there, seek him i' the other place
yourself. But indeed, if you find him not within
this month, you shall nose him as you go up the
stairs into the lobby.

King. Go seek him there.
    [*To some Attendants.*

Hamlet. He will stay till you come.

[*Exeunt Attendants.*

King. Hamlet, this deed, for thine especial safety,
    Which we do tender, as we dearly grieve
    For that which thou hast done, must send thee hence
    With fiery quickness: therefore prepare thyself;
    The bark is ready and the wind at help,
    The associates tend, and every thing is bent
    For England.

Hamlet. For England?

King. Ay, Hamlet.

Hamlet. Good.

King. So is it, if thou knew'st our purposes.

Hamlet. I see a cherub that sees them. But, come; for
    England! Farewell, dear mother.

King. Thy loving father, Hamlet.

Hamlet. My mother: father and mother is man and wife; man
    and wife is one flesh, and so, my mother. Come, for England!

[*Exit.*

King. Follow him at foot; tempt him with speed aboard;
    Delay it not; I'll have him hence to-night:
    Away! for every thing is seal'd and done
    That else leans on the affair: pray you, make haste.

        [*Exeunt Rosencrantz and Guildenstern.*

And, England, if my love thou hold'st at aught –
    As my great power thereof may give thee sense,
    Since yet thy cicatrice looks raw and red
    After the Danish sword, and thy free awe
    Pays homage to us – thou mayst not coldly set
    Our sovereign process; which imports at full,
    By letters congruing to that effect,
    The present death of Hamlet. Do it, England;
    For like the hectic in my blood he rages,
    And thou must cure me: till I know 'tis done,
    Howe'er my haps, my joys were ne'er begun.

        [*Exit.*

SCENE FOUR

A plain in Denmark.
Enter Fortinbras, *a* Captain *and* Soldiers, *marching.*

Fortinbras. Go, captain, from me greet the Danish king;
    Tell him that by his license Fortinbras
    Craves the conveyance of a promised march
    Over his kingdom. You know the rendezvous.
    If that his majesty would aught with us,
    We shall express our duty in his eye;
    And let him know so.
Captain. I will do't, my lord.
Fortinbras. Go softly on.

       [*Exeunt Fortinbras and Soldiers.*

Enter Hamlet, Rosencrantz, Guildenstern, *and others.*
Hamlet. Good sir, whose powers are these?
Captain. They are of Norway, sir.
Hamlet. How purposed, sir, I pray you?
Captain. Against some part of Poland.
Hamlet. Who commands them, sir?
Captain. The nephew to old Norway, Fortinbras.
Hamlet. Goes it against the main of Poland, sir,
    Or for some frontier?
Captain. Truly to speak, and with no addition,
    We go to gain a little patch of ground
    That hath in it no profit but the name.
    To pay five ducats, five, I would not farm it;

Nor will it yield to Norway or the Pole
 A ranker rate, should it be sold in fee.
Hamlet. Why, then the Polack never will defend it.
Captain. Yes, it is already garrison'd.
Hamlet. Two thousand souls and twenty thousand ducats
 Will not debate the question of this straw:
 This is the imposthume of much wealth and peace,
 That inward breaks, and shows no cause without
 Why the man dies. I humbly thank you, sir.
Captain. God be wi' you, sir. [*Exit.*
Rosencrantz. Will't please you go, my lord?
Hamlet. I'll be with you straight. Go a little before.

[*Exeunt all but Hamlet.*

How all occasions do inform against me,
 And spur my dull revenge! What is a man,
 If his chief good and market of his time
 Be but to sleep and feed? a beast, no more.
 Sure, he that made us with such large discourse,
 Looking before and after, gave us not
 That capability and god-like reason
 To fust in us unused. Now, whether it be
 Bestial oblivion, or some craven scruple
 Of thinking too precisely on the event, –
 A thought which, quarter'd, hath but one part wisdom
 And ever three parts coward, – I do not know
 Why yet I live to say 'this thing's to do,'
 Sith I have cause, and will, and strength, and means,
 To do't. Examples gross as earth exhort me:
 Witness this army, of such mass and charge,
 Led by a delicate and tender prince,
 Whose spirit with divine ambition puff'd
 Makes mouths at the invisible event,
 Exposing what is mortal and unsure
 To all that fortune, death and danger dare,
 Even for an egg-shell. Rightly to be great
 Is not to stir without great argument,
 But greatly to find quarrel in a straw
 When honour's at the stake. How stand I then,
 That have a father kill'd, a mother stain'd,

Excitements of my reason and my blood,
And let all sleep, while to my shame I see
The imminent death of twenty thousand men,
That for a fantasy and trick of fame
Go to their graves like beds, fight for a plot
Whereon the numbers cannot try the cause,
Which is not tomb enough and continent
To hide the slain? O, from this time forth,
My thoughts be bloody, or be nothing worth!

[*Exit.*

SCENE FIVE

Elsinore. A room in the castle.
Enter Queen, Horatio, and a Gentleman.

Queen. I will not speak with her.
Gentleman. She is importunate, indeed distract:
　Her mood will needs be pitied.
Queen. What would she have?
Gentleman. She speaks much of her father, says she hears
　There's tricks i' the world, and hems and beats her heart,
　Spurns enviously at straws; speaks things in doubt,
　That carry but half sense: her speech is nothing,
　Yet the unshaped use of it doth move
　The hearers to collection; they aim at it,
　And botch the words up fit to their own thoughts;
　Which, as her winks and nods and gestures yield them,
　Indeed would make one think there might be thought,
　Though nothing sure, yet much unhappily.
Horatio. 'Twere good she were spoken with, for she may strew
　Dangerous conjectures in ill-breeding minds.
Queen. Let her come in.

[Exit Gentleman.

[*Aside*] To my sick soul, as sin's true nature is,
Each toy seems prologue to some great amiss:
So full of artless jealousy is guilt,
It spills itself in fearing to be spilt.

Re-enter Gentleman, *with* Ophelia.

– 96 –

Ophelia. Where is the beauteous majesty of Denmark?

Queen. How now, Ophelia!

Ophelia. [*Sings*How should I your true love know
From another one? By his cockle hat and staff
And his sandal shoon.

Queen. Alas, sweet lady, what imports this song?

Ophelia. Say you? nay, pray you, mark.
[*Sings*He is dead and gone, lady,
He is dead and gone;
At his head a grass-green turf,
At his heels a stone. Oh, oh!

Queen. Nay, but, Ophelia, –

Ophelia. Pray you, mark.
[*Sings*White his shroud as the mountain snow, –

Enter King.

Queen. Alas, look here, my lord.

Ophelia. [*Sings*Larded with sweet flowers;
Which bewept to the grave did go
With true-love showers.

King. How do you, pretty lady?

Ophelia. Well, God 'ild you!
They say the owl was a baker's
Daughter. Lord, we know what we are, but know not
What we may be. God be at your table!

King. Conceit upon her father.

Ophelia. Pray you, let's have no words of this; but when they
ask you what it means, say you this:
[*Sings*To-morrow is Saint Valentine's day,
All in the morning betime,
And I a maid at your window,
To be your Valentine.
Then up he rose, and donn'd his clothes,
And dupp'd the chamber-door;
Let in the maid, that out a maid
Never departed more.

King. Pretty Ophelia!

Ophelia. Indeed, la, without an oath, I'll make an end on't:
[*Sings*By Gis and by Saint Charity,
Alack, and fie for shame!
Young men will do't, if they come to't;

By cock, they are to blame.
Quoth she, before you tumbled me,
You promised me to wed. He answers:
So would I ha' done, by yonder sun,
An thou hadst not come to my bed.
King. How long hath she been thus?
Ophelia. I hope all will be well. We must be patient: but
  I cannot choose but weep, to think they should lay him
  I' the cold ground. My brother shall know of it:
  And so I thank you for your good counsel. Come, my
  Coach! Good night, ladies; good night, sweet ladies;
  Good night, good night. [*Exit.*
King. Follow her close; give her good watch,
  I pray you.

[*Exit Horatio.*

O, this is the poison of deep grief; it springs
All from her father's death. O Gertrude, Gertrude,
When sorrows come, they come not single spies,
But in battalions! First, her father slain:
Next, your son gone; and he most violent author
Of his own just remove: the people muddied,
Thick and unwholesome in their thoughts and whispers,
For good Polonius' death; and we have done but greenly,
In hugger-mugger to inter him: poor Ophelia
Divided from herself and her fair judgement,
Without the which we are pictures, or mere beasts:
Last, and as much containing as all these,
Her brother is in secret come from France,
Feeds on his wonder, keeps himself in clouds,
And wants not buzzers to infect his ear
With pestilent speeches of his father's death;
Wherein necessity, of matter beggar'd,
Will nothing stick our person to arraign
In ear and ear. O my dear Gertrude, this,
Like to a murdering-piece, in many places
Gives me superfluous death.

[*A noise within.*

Queen. Alack, what noise is this?
King. Where are my Switzers? Let them guard the door.

Enter another Gentleman.

What is the matter?
Gentleman. Save yourself, my lord:
    The ocean, overpeering of his list,
    Eats not the flats with more impetuous haste
    Than young Laertes, in a riotous head,
    O'erbears your officers. The rabble call him lord;
    And, as the world were now but to begin,
    Antiquity forgot, custom not known,
    The ratifiers and props of every word,
    They cry 'Choose we; Laertes shall be king!'
    Caps, hands and tongues applaud it to the clouds,
    'Laertes shall be king, Laertes king!'
Queen. How cheerfully on the false trail they cry! O, this is counter,
    you false Danish dogs! [*Noise within.*
King. The doors are broke.
Enter Laertes, *armed*; Danes *following.*
Laertes. Where is this king? Sirs, stand you all without.
Danes. No, let's come in.
Laertes. I pray you, give me leave.
Danes. We will, we will.
    [*They retire without the door.*
Laertes. I thank you: keep the door. O thou vile king,
    Give me my father!
Queen. Calmly, good Laertes.
Laertes. That drop of blood that's calm proclaims me bastard;
    Cries cuckold to my father; brands the harlot
    Even here, between the chaste unsmirched brow
    Of my true mother.
King. What is the cause, Laertes,
    That thy rebellion looks so giant-like?
    Let him go, Gertrude; do not fear our person:
    There's such divinity doth hedge a king,
    That treason can but peep to what it would,
    Acts little of his will. Tell me, Laertes,
    Why thou art thus incensed: let him go, Gertrude:
    Speak, man.

Laertes. Where is my father?

King. Dead.

Queen. But not by him.

King. Let him demand his fill.

Laertes. How came he dead? I'll not be juggled with:
    To hell, allegiance! vows, to the blackest devil!
    Conscience and grace, to the profoundest pit!
    I dare damnation: to this point I stand,
    That both the worlds I give to negligence,
    Let come what comes; only I'll be revenged
    Most throughly for my father.

King. Who shall stay you?

Laertes. My will, not all the world:
    And for my means, I'll husband them so well,
    They shall go far with little.

King. Good Laertes,
    If you desire to know the certainty
    Of your dear father's death, is't writ in your revenge,
    That, swoopstake, you will draw both friend and foe,
    Winner and loser?

Laertes. None but his enemies.

King. Will you know them then?

Laertes. To his good friends thus wide I'll ope my arms;
    And, like the kind life-rendering pelican,
    Repast them with my blood.

King. Why, now you speak
    Like a good child and a true gentleman.
    That I am guiltless of your father's death,
    And am most sensibly in grief for it,
    It shall as level to your judgement pierce
    As day does to your eye.

Danes. [*Within*Let her come in.

Laertes. How now! what noise is that?

Re-enter Ophelia.

    O heat, dry up my brains! tears seven times salt,
    Burn out the sense and virtue of mine eye!
    By heaven, thy madness shall be paid with weight,
    Till our scale turn the beam. O rose of May!
    Dear maid, kind sister, sweet Ophelia!

O heavens! is't possible a young maid's wits
Should be as mortal as an old man's life?
Nature is fine in love, and where 'tis fine
It sends some precious instance of itself
After the thing it loves.
Ophelia. [*Sings*
They bore him barefaced on the bier;
Hey non nonny, nonny, hey nonny:
And in his grave rain'd many a tear, –
Fare you well, my dove!
Laertes. Hadst thou thy wits, and didst persuade revenge,
It could not move thus.
Ophelia. [*Sings*
You must sing down a-down,
An you call him a-down-a.
O, how the wheel becomes it! It is the false
Steward, that stole his master's daughter.
Laertes. This nothing's more than matter.
Ophelia. There's rosemary, that's for remembrance: pray you,
Love, remember: and there is pansies, that's for thoughts.
Laertes. A document in madness; thoughts and remembrance fitted.
Ophelia. There's fennel for you, and columbines: there's rue
For you; and here's some for me: we may call it
Herb of grace o' Sundays: O, you must wear your rue with
A difference. There's a daisy: I would give you
Some violets, but they withered all when my father
Died: they say a' made a good end, –
[*Sings*
For bonny sweet Robin is all my joy.

Laertes. Thought and affliction, passion, hell itself,
She turns to favour and to prettiness.
Ophelia. [*Sings*And will a' not come again?
And will a' not come again?
No, no, he is dead,
Go to thy death-bed,
He never will come again.
His beard was as white as snow,
All flaxen was his poll:
He is gone, he is gone,
And we cast away moan:

God ha' mercy on his soul!
And of all Christian souls, I pray God.
God be wi' you.

[*Exit.*

Laertes. Do you see this, O God?
King. Laertes, I must commune with your grief,
 Or you deny me right. Go but apart,
 Make choice of whom your wisest friends you will,
 And they shall hear and judge 'twixt you and me:
 If by direct or by collateral hand
 They find us touch'd, we will our kingdom give,
 Our crown, our life, and all that we call ours,
 To you in satisfaction; but if not,
 Be you content to lend your patience to us,
 And we shall jointly labour with your soul
 To give it due content.
Laertes. Let this be so;
 His means of death, his obscure funeral,
 No trophy, sword, nor hatchment o'er his bones,
 No noble rite nor formal ostentation,
 Cry to be heard, as 'twere from heaven to earth,
 That I must call't in question.
King. So you shall;
 And where the offence is let the great axe fall.
 I pray you, go with me.

[*Exeunt.*

SCENE SIX

Another room in the castle.
Enter Horatio *and a* Servant.

Horatio. What are they that would speak with me?
Servant. Sea-faring men, sir: they say they have letters for you.
Horatio. Let them come in.

[*Exit Servant.*

I do not know from what part of the world
I should be greeted, if not from Lord Hamlet.

Enter Sailors.

First Sailor. God bless you, sir.
Horatio. Let him bless thee too.
First Sailor. He shall, sir, an't please him.
There's a letter for
You, sir; it comes from the ambassador that was
Bound for England; if your name be Horatio, as I am
Let to know it is.
Horatio. [*Reads*] 'Horatio, when thou shalt have over-looked
this, give these fellows some means to the king:
they have letters for him. Ere we were two days old
at sea, a pirate of very warlike appointment gave us
chase. Finding ourselves too slow of sail, we put on
a compelled valour: and in the grapple I boarded
them: on the instant they got clear of our ship; so
I alone became their prisoner. They have dealt with

ROYAL CLASSICS | *Hamlet*

me like thieves of mercy: but they knew what they
did; I am to do a good turn for them. Let the king
have the letters I have sent; and repair thou to me
with as much speed as thou wouldest fly death.
I have words to speak in thine ear will make thee
dumb; yet are they much too light for the bore of
the matter. These good fellows will bring thee
where I am. Rosencrantz and Guildenstern hold their
course for England: of them I have much to tell
thee. Farewell.
'He that thou knowest thine, Hamlet.'
Come, I will make you way for these your letters;
And do't the speedier, that you may direct me
To him from whom you brought them.

[*Exeunt.*

SCENE SEVEN

Another room in the castle.
Enter King *and* Laertes.

King. Now must your conscience my acquittance seal,
 And you must put me in your heart for friend,
 Sith you have heard, and with a knowing ear,
 That he which hath your noble father slain
 Pursued my life.
Laertes. It well appears: but tell me
 Why you proceeded not against these feats,
 So crimeful and so capital in nature,
 As by your safety, wisdom, all things else,
 You mainly were stirr'd up.
King. O, for two special reasons,
 Which may to you perhaps seem much unsinew'd,
 But yet to me they're strong. The queen his mother
 Lives almost by his looks; and for myself –
 My virtue or my plague, be it either which –
 She's so conjunctive to my life and soul,
 That, as the star moves not but in his sphere,
 I could not but by her. The other motive,
 Why to a public count I might not go,
 Is the great love the general gender bear him;
 Who, dipping all his faults in their affection,
 Would, like the spring that turneth wood to stone,
 Convert his gyves to graces; so that my arrows,
 Too slightly timber'd for so loud a wind,
 Would have reverted to my bow again
 And not where I had aim'd them.

Laertes. And so have I a noble father lost;
  A sister driven into desperate terms,
  Whose worth, if praises may go back again,
  Stood challenger on mount of all the age
  For her perfections: but my revenge will come.
King. Break not your sleeps for that: you must not think
  That we are made of stuff so flat and dull
  That we can let our beard be shook with danger
  And think it pastime. You shortly shall hear more:
  I loved your father, and we love ourself;
  And that, I hope, will teach you to imagine –

Enter a Messenger, *with letters.*

How now! what news?
Messenger. Letters, my lord, from Hamlet:
  This to your majesty; this to the queen.
King. From Hamlet! who brought them?
Messenger. Sailors, my lord, they say; I saw them not:
  They were given me by Claudio; he received them
  Of him that brought them.
King. Laertes, you shall hear them. Leave us.

[Exit Messenger.

[*Reads*] 'High and mighty,
  You shall know I am set naked on
  your kingdom. To-morrow shall I beg leave to see
  your kingly eyes: when I shall, first asking your
  pardon thereunto, recount the occasion of my sudden
  and more strange return. 'Hamlet.' What should this mean?
  Are all the rest come back?
  Or is it some abuse, and no such thing?
Laertes. Know you the hand?
King. Tis Hamlet's character. 'Naked!'
  And in a postscript here, he says 'alone.'
  Can you advise me?
Laertes. I'm lost in it, my lord. But let him come;
  It warms the very sickness in my heart,
  That I shall live and tell him to his teeth,
  'Thus didest thou.'

King. If it be so, Laertes, –
    As how should it be so? how otherwise? –
    Will you be ruled by me?
Laertes. Ay, my lord;
    So you will not o'errule me to a peace.
King. To thine own peace. If he be now return'd,
    As checking at his voyage, and that he means
    No more to undertake it, I will work him
    To an exploit now ripe in my device,
    Under the which he shall not choose but fall:
    And for his death no wind of blame shall breathe;
    But even his mother shall uncharge the practice,
    And call it accident.
Laertes. My lord, I will be ruled;
    The rather, if you could devise it so
    That I might be the organ.
King. It falls right.
    You have been talk'd of since your travel much,
    And that in Hamlet's hearing, for a quality
    Wherein, they say, you shine: your sum of parts
    Did not together pluck such envy from him,
    As did that one, and that in my regard
    Of the unworthiest siege.
Laertes. What part is that, my lord?
King. A very riband in the cap of youth,
    Yet needful too; for youth no less becomes
    The light and careless livery that it wears
    Than settled age his sables and his weeds,
    Importing health and graveness. Two months since,
    Here was a gentleman of Normandy: –
    I've seen myself, and served against, the French,
    And they can well on horseback: but this gallant
    Had witchcraft in't; he grew unto his seat,
    And to such wondrous doing brought his horse
    As had he been incorpsed and demi-natured
    With the brave beast: so far he topp'd my thought
    That I, in forgery of shapes and tricks,
    Come short of what he did.
Laertes. A Norman was't?
King. A Norman.
Laertes. Upon my life, Lamond.

King. The very same.

Laertes. I know him well: he is the brooch indeed
 And gem of all the nation.

King. He made confession of you,
 And gave you such a masterly report,
 For art and exercise in your defence,
 And for your rapier most especial,
 That he cried out, 'twould be a sight indeed
 If one could match you: the scrimers of their nation.
 He swore, had neither motion, guard, nor eye,
 If you opposed them. Sir, this report of his
 Did Hamlet so envenom with his envy
 That he could nothing do but wish and beg
 Your sudden coming o'er, to play with him.
 Now, out of this –

Laertes. What out of this, my lord?

King. Laertes, was your father dear to you?
 Or are you like the painting of a sorrow,
 A face without a heart?

Laertes. Why ask you this?

King. Not that I think you did not love your father,
 But that I know love is begun by time,
 And that I see, in passages of proof,
 Time qualifies the spark and fire of it.
 There lives within the very flame of love
 A kind of wick or snuff that will abate it;
 And nothing is at a like goodness still,
 For goodness, growing to a plurisy,
 Dies in his own too much: that we would do
 We should do when we would; for this 'would' changes
 And hath abatements and delays as many
 As there are tongues, are hands, are accidents,
 And then this 'should' is like a spendthrift sigh,
 That hurts by easing. But, to the quick o' the ulcer:
 Hamlet comes back: what would you undertake,
 To show yourself your father's son in deed
 More than in words?

Laertes. To cut his throat i' the church.

King. No place indeed should murder sanctuarize;
 Revenge should have no bounds. But, good Laertes,
 Will you do this, keep close within your chamBernardo.

Hamlet return'd shall know you are come home:
We'll put on those shall praise your excellence
And set a double varnish on the fame
The Frenchman gave you; bring you in fine together
And wager on your heads: he, being remiss,
Most generous and free from all contriving,
Will not peruse the foils, so that with ease,
Or with a little shuffling, you may choose
A sword unbated, and in a pass of practice
Requite him for your father.
Laertes. I will do't And for that purpose I'll anoint my sword.
  I bought an unction of a mountebank,
  So mortal that but dip a knife in it,
  Where it draws blood no cataplasm so rare,
  Collected from all simples that have virtue
  Under the moon, can save the thing from death
  That is but scratch'd withal: I'll touch my point
  With this contagion, that, if I gall him slightly,
  It may be death.
King. Let's further think of this;
  Weigh what convenience both of time and means
  May fit us to our shape: if this should fail,
  And that our drift look through our bad performance,
  'Twere better not assay'd: therefore this project
  Should have a back or second, that might hold
  If this did blast in proof. Soft! let me see:
  We'll make a solemn wager on your cunnings: I ha't:
  When in your motion you are hot and dry –
  As make your bouts more violent to that end –
  And that he calls for drink, I'll have prepared him
  A chalice for the nonce; whereon but sipping,
  If he by chance escape your venom'd stuck,
  Our purpose may hold there.
  But stay, what noise?

Enter Queen.

  How now, sweet queen!
Queen. One woe doth tread upon another's heel,
  So fast they follow: your sister's drown'd, Laertes.
Laertes. Drown'd! O, where?

Queen. There is a willow grows aslant a brook,
That shows his hoar leaves in the glassy stream;
There with fantastic garlands did she come
Of crow-flowers, nettles, daisies, and long purples,
That liberal shepherds give a grosser name,
But our cold maids do dead men's fingers call them:
There, on the pendent boughs her coronet weeds
Clambering to hang, an envious sliver broke;
When down her weedy trophies and herself
Fell in the weeping brook. Her clothes spread wide,
And mermaid-like awhile they bore her up:
Which time she chanted snatches of old tunes,
As one incapable of her own distress,
Or like a creature native and indued
Unto that element: but long it could not be
Till that her garments, heavy with their drink,
Pull'd the poor wretch from her melodious lay
To muddy death.
Laertes. Alas, then she is drown'd!
Queen. Drown'd, drown'd.
Laertes. Too much of water hast thou, poor Ophelia,
And therefore I forbid my tears: but yet
It is our trick; nature her custom holds,
Let shame say what it will: when these are gone,
The woman will be out. Adieu, my lord:
I have a speech of fire that fain would blaze,
But that this folly douts it.

[*Exit.*

King. Let's follow, Gertrude:
How much I had to do to calm his rage!
Now fear I this will give it start again;
Therefore let's follow.

[*Exeunt.*

Act V.

A churchyard.
Enter two Clowns, *with spades, & c.*

First Clown. Is she to be buried in Christian burial that
    Wilfully seeks her own salvation?
Second Clown. I tell thee she is; and therefore make her grave
    Straight: the crowner hath sat on her, and finds it
    Christian burial.
First Clown. How can that be, unless she drowned herself in her
    Own defence?
Second Clown. Why, 'tis found so.
First Clown. It must be 'se offendendo;' it cannot be else. For
    Here lies the point: if I drown myself wittingly,
    It argues an act: and an act hath three branches; it
    Is, to act, to do, and to perform: argal, she drowned
    Herself wittingly.
Second Clown. Nay, but hear you, goodman delver.
First Clown. Give me leave. Here lies the water; good: here
    Stands the man; good: if the man go to this water
    And drown himself, it is, will he, nill he, he
    Goes; mark you that; but if the water come to him
    And drown him, he drowns not himself: argal, he
    That is not guilty of his own death shortens not his own life.
Second Clown. But is this law?
First Clown. Ay, marry, is't; crowner's quest law.
Second Clown. Will you ha' the truth on't? If this had not been
    A gentlewoman, she should have been buried out o'
    Christian burial.

First Clown. Why, there thou say'st: and the more pity that
　　Great folk should have countenance in this world to
　　Drown or hang themselves, more than their even
　　Christian. Come, my spade. There is no ancient
　　Gentlemen but gardeners, ditchers and grave-makers:
　　They hold up Adam's profession.
Second Clown. Was he a gentleman?
First Clown. A' was the first that ever bore arms.
Second Clown. Why, he had none.
First Clown. What, art a heathen? How dost thou underStand the
　　Scripture? The
　　Scripture says Adam digged:
　　Could he dig without arms? I'll put another
　　Question to thee: if thou answerest me not to the
　　Purpose, confess thyself –
Second Clown. Go to.
First Clown. What is he that builds stronger than either the
　　Mason, the shipwright, or the carpenter?
Second Clown. The gallows-maker; for that frame outlives a
　　Thousand tenants.
First Clown. I like thy wit well, in good faith: the gallows
　　Does well; but how does it well? it does well to
　　Those that do ill: now, thou dost ill to say the
　　Gallows is built stronger than the church: argal,
　　The gallows may do well to thee. To't again, come.
Second Clown. 'Who builds stronger than a mason, a shipwright, or
　　A carpenter?'
First Clown. Ay, tell me that, and unyoke.
Second Clown. Marry, now I can tell.
First Clown. To't.
Second Clown. Mass, I cannot tell.

Enter Hamlet *and* Horatio, *afar off.*

First Clown. Cudgel thy brains no more about it, for your dull
　　Ass will not mend his pace with beating, and when
　　You are asked this question next, say 'a
　　Grave-maker:' the houses that he makes last till
　　Doomsday. Go, get thee to Yaughan; fetch me a
　　Stoup of liquor.

William Shakespeare

[*Exit Second Clown.*
[*He digs, and sings.*

In youth, when I did love, did love,
Methought it was very sweet,
To contract, O, the time, for-a my behove,
O, methought, there-a was nothing-a meet.
Hamlet. Has this fellow no feeling of his business, that he
Sings at grave-making?
Horatio. Custom hath made it in him a property of easiness.
Hamlet. 'Tis e'en so: the hand of little employment hath
The daintier sense.
First Clown. [*Sings* But age, with his stealing steps,
Hath claw'd me in his clutch,
And hath shipped me intil the land,
As if I had never been such.
[*Throws up a skull.*
Hamlet. That skull had a tongue in it, and could sing once:
How the knave jowls it to the ground, as if it were
Cain's jaw-bone, that did the first murder! It
Might be the pate of a politician, which this ass
Now o'er-reaches; one that would circumvent God,
Might it not?
Horatio. It might, my lord.
Hamlet. Or of a courtier, which could say 'Good morrow,
Sweet lord! How dost thou, sweet lord?' This might
Be my lord such-a-one, that praised my lord
Such-a-one's horse, when he meant to beg it; might it Not?
Horatio. Ay, my lord.
Hamlet. Why, e'en so: and now my Lady Worm's; chapless, and
Knocked about the mazzard with a sexton's spade:
Here's fine revolution, an we had the trick to
See't. Did these bones cost no more the breeding,
But to play at loggats with 'em? mine ache to think on't.
First Clown. [*Sings*
A pick-axe, and a spade, a spade,
For and a shrouding sheet:
O, a pit of clay for to be made
For such a guest is meet.

[Throws up another skull.

Hamlet. There's another: why may not that be the skull of a
Lawyer? Where be his quiddities now, his quillets,
His cases, his tenures, and his tricks? why does he
Suffer this rude knave now to knock him about the
Sconce with a dirty shovel, and will not tell him of
His action of battery? Hum! This fellow might be
In's time a great buyer of land, with his statutes,
His recognizances, his fines, his double vouchers,
His recoveries: is this the fine of his fines and
The recovery of his recoveries, to have his fine
Pate full of fine dirt? will his vouchers vouch him
No more of his purchases, and double ones too, than
The length and breadth of a pair of indentures? The
Very conveyances of his lands will hardly lie in
This box; and must the inheritor himself have no more, ha?
Horatio. Not a jot more, my lord.
Hamlet. Is not parchment made of sheep-skins?
Horatio. Ay, my lord, and of calf-skins too.
Hamlet. They are sheep and calves which seek out assurance
    In that. I will speak to this fellow. Whose
    Grave's this, sirrah?
First Clown. Mine, sir.
    [*Sings*
    O, a pit of clay for to be made
    For such a guest is meet.
Hamlet. I think it be thine indeed, for thou liest in't.
First Clown. You lie out on't, sir, and therefore 'tis not
    Yours: for my part, I do not lie in't, and yet it is mine.
Hamlet. Thou dost lie in't, to be in't and say it is thine:
    'Tis for the dead, not for the quick; therefore thou liest.
First Clown. 'Tis a quick lie, sir; 'twill away again, from me to you.
Hamlet. What man dost thou dig it for?
First Clown. For no man, sir.
Hamlet. What woman then?
First Clown. For none, neither.
Hamlet. Who is to be buried in 't?
First Clown. One that was a woman, sir; but, rest her soul, she's
    dead.
Hamlet. How absolute the knave is! we must speak by the
    Card, or equivocation will undo us. By the Lord,
    Horatio, this three years I have taken note of

It; the age is grown so picked that the toe of the
Peasant comes so near the heel of the courtier, he
Galls his kibe. How long hast thou been a
Grave-maker?

First Clown. Of all the days i' the year, I came to't that day
    That our last king Hamlet o'ercame Fortinbras.

Hamlet. How long is that since?

First Clown. Cannot you tell that? every fool can tell that: it
    Was that very day that young Hamlet was born; he that
    Is mad, and sent into England.

Hamlet. Ay, marry, why was he sent into England?

First Clown. Why, because a' was mad: a' shall recover his wits
    There; or, if a' do not, 'tis no great matter there.

Hamlet. Why?

First Clown. 'Twill not be seen in him there; there the men
    Are as mad as he.

Hamlet. How came he mad?

First Clown. Very strangely, they say.

Hamlet. How 'strangely'?

First Clown. Faith, e'en with losing his wits.

Hamlet. Upon what ground?

First Clown. Why, here in Denmark: I have been sexton here, man
    And boy, thirty years.

Hamlet. How long will a man lie i' the earth ere he rot?

First Clown. I'faith, if a' be not rotten before a' die – as we
    Have many pocky corses now-a-days, that will scarce
    Hold the laying in – a' will last you some eight year
    Or nine year: a tanner will last you nine year.

Hamlet. Why he more than another?

First Clown. Why, sir, his hide is so tanned with his trade that
    A' will keep out water a great while; and your water
    Is a sore decayer of your whoreson dead body.
    Here's a skull now: this skull has lain in the earth
    Three and twenty years.

Hamlet. Whose was it?

First Clown. A whoreson mad fellow's it was: whose do you think it
    was?

Hamlet. Nay, I know not.

First Clown. A pestilence on him for a mad rogue! a' poured a
    Flagon of Rhenish on my head once. This same skull,
    Sir, was Yorick's skull, the king's jester.

Hamlet. This?
First Clown. E'en that.
Hamlet. Let me see.

[*Takes the skull.*]

Alas, poor Yorick! I knew him, Horatio: a fellow
Of infinite jest, of most excellent fancy: he hath
Borne me on his back a thousand times; and now how
Abhorred in my imagination it is! my gorge rises at
It. Here hung those lips that I have kissed I know
Not how oft. Where be your gibes now? your
Gambols? your songs? your flashes of merriment,
That were wont to set the table on a roar? Not one
Now, to mock your own grinning? quite chop-fallen?
Now get you to my lady's chamber, and tell her, let
Her paint an inch thick, to this favour she must
Come; make her laugh at that. Prithee, Horatio, tell
Me one thing.
Horatio. What's that, my lord?
Hamlet. Dost thou think Alexander looked o' this fashion i'
The earth?
Horatio. E'en so.
Hamlet. And smelt so? pah!

[*Puts down the skull.*

Horatio. E'en so, my lord.
Hamlet. To what base uses we may return, Horatio! Why may
Not imagination trace the noble dust of Alexander,
Till he find it stopping a bung-hole?
Horatio. 'Twere to consider too curiously, to consider so.
Hamlet. No, faith, not a jot; but to follow him thither with
Modesty enough and likelihood to lead it: as
Thus: Alexander died, Alexander was buried,
Alexander returneth into dust; the dust is earth; of
Earth we make loam; and why of that loam, whereto he
Was converted, might they not stop a beer-barrel?
Imperious Cæsar, dead and turn'd to clay,
Might stop a hole to keep the wind away:
O, that that earth, which kept the world in awe,

Should patch a wall to expel the winter's flaw!
But soft! but soft! aside: here comes the king.

> *Enter* Priests, *&c. in procession;*
> *the Corpse of Ophelia,* Laertes *and* Mourners *following;*
> King, Queen, *their trains, &c.*

The queen, the courtiers: who is this they follow?
And with such maimed rites? This doth betoken
The corse they follow did with desperate hand
Fordo its own life: 'twas of some estate.
Couch we awhile, and mark.
[*Retiring with Horatio.*
Laertes. What ceremony else?
Hamlet. That is Laertes, a very noble youth: mark.
Laertes. What ceremony else?
First Priest. Her obsequies have been as far enlarged
    As we have warranty: her death was doubtful;
    And, but that great command o'ersways the order,
    She should in ground unsanctified have lodged
    Till the last trumpet; for charitable prayers,
    Shards, flints and pebbles should be thrown on her:
    Yet here she is allow'd her virgin crants,
    Her maiden strewments and the bringing home
    Of bell and burial.
Laertes. Must there no more be done?
First Priest. No more be done:
    We should profane the service of the dead
    To sing a requiem and such rest to her
    As to peace-parted souls.
Laertes. Lay her i' the earth:
    And from her fair and unpolluted flesh
    May violets spring! I tell thee, churlish priest,
    A ministering angel shall my sister be,
    When thou liest howling.
Hamlet. What, the fair Ophelia!
Queen. [*Scattering flowers*]
    Sweets to the sweet: farewell!
    I hoped thou shouldst have been my Hamlet's wife;
    I thought thy bride-bed to have deck'd, sweet maid,
    And not have strew'd thy grave.

Laertes. O, treble woe
    Fall ten times treble on that cursed head
    Whose wicked deed thy most ingenious sense
    Deprived thee of! Hold off the earth awhile,
    Till I have caught her once more in mine arms:
    [*Leaps into the grave.*
Now pile your dust upon the quick and dead,
    Till of this flat a mountain you have made
    To o'ertop old Pelion or the skyish head
    Of blue Olympus.
Hamlet. [*Advancing*] What is he whose grief
    Bears such an emphasis? whose phrase of sorrow
    Conjures the wandering stars and makes them stand
    Like wonder-wounded hearers? This is I,
    Hamlet the Dane. [*Leaps into the grave.*
Laertes. The devil take thy soul!

                [*Grappling with him.*

Hamlet. Thou pray'st not well.
    I prithee, take thy fingers from my throat;
    For, though I am not splenitive and rash,
    Yet have I in me something dangerous,
    Which let thy wisdom fear.
    Hold off thy hand.
King. Pluck them asunder.
Queen. Hamlet, Hamlet!
All. Gentlemen, –
Horatio. Good my lord, be quiet.

          [*The Attendants part them,*
        and they come out of the grave.

Hamlet. Why, I will fight with him upon this theme
    Until my eyelids will no longer wag.
Queen. O my son, what theme?
Hamlet. I loved Ophelia: forty thousand brothers
    Could not, with all their quantity of love,
    Make up my sum. What wilt thou do for her?
King. O, he is mad, Laertes.
Queen. For love of God, forbear him.

Hamlet. 'Swounds, show me what thou'lt do:
  Woo't weep? woo't fight? woo't fast? woo't tear thyself?
  Woo't drink up eisel? eat a crocodile?
  I'll do't. Dost thou come here to whine?
  To outface me with leaping in her grave?
  Be buried quick with her, and so will I:
  And, if thou prate of mountains, let them throw
  Millions of acres on us, till our ground,
  Singeing his pate against the burning zone,
  Make Ossa like a wart! Nay, an thou'lt mouth,
  I'll rant as well as thou.
Queen. This is mere madness:
  And thus awhile the fit will work on him;
  Anon, as patient as the female dove
  When that her golden couplets are disclosed,
  His silence will sit drooping.
Hamlet. Hear you, sir;
  What is the reason that you use me thus?
  I loved you ever: but it is no matter;
  Let Hercules himself do what he may,
  The cat will mew, and dog will have his day.

[*Exit.*

King. I pray thee, good Horatio, wait upon him.

[*Exit Horatio.*

[*To Laertes*]
Strengthen your patience in our last night's speech;
We'll put the matter to the present push.
Good Gertrude, set some watch over your son.
This grave shall have a living monument:
An hour of quiet shortly shall we see;
Till then, in patience our proceeding be.

[*Exeunt.*

SCENE TWO

A hall in the castle.
Enter Hamlet *and* Horatio.

Hamlet. So much for this, sir: now shall you see the other;
    You do remember all the circumstance?
Horatio. Remember it, my lord!
Hamlet. Sir, in my heart there was a kind of fighting,
    That would not let me sleep: methought I lay
    Worse than the mutines in the bilboes. Rashly,
    And praised be rashness for it, let us know,
    Our indiscretion sometime serves us well
    When our deep plots do pall; and that should learn us
    There's a divinity that shapes our ends,
    Rough-hew them how we will.
Horatio. That is most certain.
Hamlet. Up from my cabin,
    My sea-gown scarf'd about me, in the dark
    Groped I to find out them; had my desire,
    Finger'd their packet, and in fine withdrew
    To mine own room again; making so bold,
    My fears forgetting manners, to unseal
    Their grand commission; where I found, Horatio, –
    O royal knavery! – an exact command,
    Larded with many several sorts of reasons,
    Importing Denmark's health and England's too,
    With, ho! such bugs and goblins in my life,
    That, on the supervise, no leisure bated,
    No, not to stay the grinding of the axe,
    My head should be struck off.

Horatio. Is't possible?
Hamlet. Here's the commission: read it at more leisure.
    But wilt thou hear now how I did proceed?
Horatio. I beseech you.
Hamlet. Being thus be-netted round with villanies, –
    Or I could make a prologue to my brains,
    They had begun the play, – I sat me down;
    Devised a new commission; wrote it fair:
    I once did hold it, as our statists do,
    A baseness to write fair, and labour'd much
    How to forget that learning; but, sir, now
    It did me yeoman's service: wilt thou know
    The effect of what I wrote?
Horatio. Ay, good my lord.
Hamlet. An earnest conjuration from the king,
    As England was his faithful tributary,
    As love between them like the palm might flourish,
    As peace should still her wheaten garland wear
    And stand a comma 'tween their amities,
    And many such-like 'As'es of great charge,
    That, on the view and knowing of these contents,
    Without debatement further, more or less,
    He should the bearers put to sudden death,
    Not shriving-time allow'd.
Horatio. How was this seal'd?
Hamlet. Why, even in that was heaven ordinant.
    I had my father's signet in my purse,
    Which was the model of that Danish seal:
    Folded the writ up in the form of the other;
    Subscribed it; gave't the impression; placed it safely,
    The changeling never known. Now, the next day
    Was our sea-fight; and what to this was sequent
    Thou know'st already.
Horatio. So Guildenstern and Rosencrantz go to't.
Hamlet. Why, man, they did make love to this employment;
    They are not near my conscience; their defeat
    Does by their own insinuation grow:
    'Tis dangerous when the baser nature comes
    Between the pass and fell incensed points
    Of mighty opposites.
Horatio. Why, what a king is this!

Hamlet. Does it not, thinks't thee, stand me now upon –
 He that hath kill'd my king, and whored my mother;
 Popp'd in between the election and my hopes;
 Thrown out his angle for my proper life,
 And with such cozenage – is't not perfect conscience,
 To quit him with this arm? and is't not to be damn'd,
 To let this canker of our nature come
 In further evil?
Horatio. It must be shortly known to him from England
 What is the issue of the business there.
Hamlet. It will be short: the interim is mine;
 And a man's life's no more than to say 'One.'
 But I am very sorry, good Horatio,
 That to Laertes I forgot myself;
 For, by the image of my cause, I see
 The portraiture of his: I'll court his favours:
 But, sure, the bravery of his grief did put me
 Into a towering passion.
Horatio. Peace! who comes here?
Enter Osric.
Osric. Your lordship is right welcome back to Denmark.
Hamlet. I humbly thank you, sir. Dost know this water-fly?
Horatio. No, my good lord.
Hamlet. Thy state is the more gracious, for 'tis a vice to
 Know him. He hath much land, and fertile: let a
 Beast be lord of beasts, and his crib shall stand at
 The king's mess: 'tis a chough, but, as I say,
 Spacious in the possession of dirt.
Osric. Sweet lord, if your lordship were at leisure, I
 should impart a thing to you from his majesty.
Hamlet. I will receive it, sir, with all diligence of
 Spirit. Put your bonnet to his right use; 'tis for the head.
Osric. I thank your lordship, it is very hot.
Hamlet. No, believe me, 'tis very cold; the wind is northerly.
Osric. It is indifferent cold, my lord, indeed.
Hamlet. But yet methinks it is very sultry and hot, or my
 Complexion –
Osric. Exceedingly, my lord; it is very sultry, as
 'Twere, – I cannot tell how. But, my lord, his
 Majesty bade me signify to you that he has laid a
 Great wager on your head: sir, this is the matter –

Hamlet. I beseech you, remember –
[*Hamlet moves him to put on his hat.*
Osric. Nay, good my lord; for mine ease, in good faith.
   Sir, here is newly come to court Laertes; believe
   Me, an absolute gentleman, full of most excellent
   Differences, of very soft society and great showing:
   Indeed, to speak feelingly of him, he is the card or
   Calendar of gentry, for you shall find in him the
   Continent of what part a gentleman would see.
Hamlet. Sir, his definement suffers no perdition in you;
   Though, I know, to divide him inventorially would
   Dizzy the arithmetic of memory, and yet but yaw
   Neither, in respect of his quick Sailor. But in the
   Verity of extolment, I take him to be a soul of
   Great article, and his infusion of such dearth and
   Rareness, as, to make true diction of him, his
   Semblable is his mirror, and who else would trace
   Him, his umbrage, nothing more.
Osric. Your lordship speaks most infallibly of him.
Hamlet. The concernancy, sir?
   Why do we wrap the gentleman
   In our more rawer breath?
Osric. Sir?
Horatio. Is't not possible to understand in another tongue?
   You will do't, sir, really.
Hamlet. What imports the nomination of this gentleman?
Osric. Of Laertes?
Horatio. His purse is empty already; all's golden words are spent.
Hamlet. Of him, sir.
Osric. I know you are not ignorant –
Hamlet. I would you did, sir; yet, in faith, if you did,
   It would not much approve me. Well, sir?
Osric. You are not ignorant of what excellence Laertes is –
Hamlet. I dare not confess that, lest I should compare with
   Him in excellence; but, to know a man well, were to
   Know himself.
Osric. I mean, sir, for his weapon; but in the imputation
   Laid on him by them, in his meed he's unfellowed.
Hamlet. What's his weapon?
Osric. Rapier and dagger.
Hamlet. That's two of his weapons: but, well.

Osric. The king, sir, hath wagered with him six Barbary
    Horses: against the which he has imponed, as I take
    It, six French rapiers and poniards, with their
    Assigns, as girdle, hanger, and so: three of the
    Carriages, in faith, are very dear to fancy, very
    Responsive to the hilts, most delicate carriages,
    And of very liberal conceit.
Hamlet. What call you the carriages?
Horatio. I knew you must be edified by the margent ere you had done.
Osric. The carriages, sir, are the hangers.
Hamlet. The phrase would be more germane to the matter if we
    Could carry a cannon by our sides: I would it might
    Be hangers till then. But, on: six Barbary horses
    Against six French swords, their assigns, and three
    Liberal-conceited carriages; that's the French bet
    Against the Danish. Why is this 'imponed,' as you call it?
Osric. The king, sir, hath laid, sir, that in a dozen passes
    Between yourself and him, he shall not exceed you
    Three hits: he hath laid on twelve for nine; and it
    Would come to immediate trial, if your lordship
    Would vouchsafe the answer.
Hamlet. How if I answer 'no'?
Osric. I mean, my lord, the opposition of your person in trial.
Hamlet. Sir, I will walk here in the hall: if it please his
    Majesty, it is the breathing time of day with me; let
    The foils be brought, the gentleman willing, and the
    King hold his purpose, I will win for him an I can;
    If not, I will gain nothing but my shame and the odd hits.
Osric. Shall I redeliver you e'en so?
Hamlet. To this effect, sir, after what flourish your nature will.
Osric. I commend my duty to your lordship.
Hamlet. Yours, yours.

[*Exit Osric.*]

    He does well to commend it himself; there are no
    Tongues else for's turn.
Horatio. This lapwing runs away with the shell on his head.
Hamlet. He did comply with his dug before he sucked it.
    Thus has he – and many more of the same breed that I
    Know the drossy age dotes on – only got the tune of

The time and outward habit of encounter; a kind of
Yesty collection, which carries them through and
Through the most fond and winnowed opinions; and do
But blow them to their trial, the bubbles are out.

Enter a Lord.

Lord. My lord, his majesty commended him to you by young
    Osric, who brings back to him, that you attend him in
    The hall: he sends to know if your pleasure hold to
    Play with Laertes, or that you will take longer time.
Hamlet. I am constant to my purposes; they follow the king's
    Pleasure: if his fitness speaks, mine is ready; now
    Or whensoever, provided I be so able as now.
Lord. The king and queen and all are coming down.
Hamlet. In happy time.
Lord. The queen desires you to use some gentle
    Entertainment to Laertes before you fall to play.
Hamlet. She well instructs me.
    [*Exit Lord.*
Horatio. You will lose this wager, my lord.
Hamlet. I do not think so; since he went into France, I
    Have been in continual practice; I shall win at the
    Odds. But thou wouldst not think how ill all's here
    About my heart: but it is no matter.
Horatio. Nay, good my lord, –
Hamlet. It is but foolery; but it is such a kind of
    Gain-giving as would perhaps trouble a woman.
Horatio. If your mind dislike any thing, obey it. I will
    Forestal their repair hither, and say you are not
    Fit.
Hamlet. Not a whit; we defy augury: there is special
    Providence in the fall of a sparrow. If it be now, 'tis not to come;
    If it be not to come, it will be now; if it be not
    Now, yet it will come: the readiness is all; since no man
    Has aught of what he leaves, what is't to leave betimes? Let be.

Enter King, Queen, Laertes, *and* Lords,
Osric *and other* Attendants *with foils and gauntlets;
a table and flagons of wine on it.*

King. Come, Hamlet, come, and take this hand from me.

[*The King puts Laertes' hand into Hamlet's.*

Hamlet. Give me your pardon, sir: I've done you wrong;
    But pardon't, as you are a gentleman.
    This presence knows,
    And you must needs have heard, how I am punish'd
    With sore distraction. What I have done,
    That might your nature, honour and exception Roughly awake, I
    Here proclaim was madness.
    Was't Hamlet wrong'd Laertes? Never Hamlet:
    If Hamlet from himself be ta'en away,
    And when he's not himself does wrong Laertes,
    Then Hamlet does it not, Hamlet denies it.
    Who does it then? His madness: if't be so,
    Hamlet is of the faction that is wrong'd;
    His madness is poor Hamlet's enemy.
    Sir, in this audience,
    Let my disclaiming from a purposed evil
    Free me so far in your most generous thoughts,
    That I have shot mine arrow o'er the house,
    And hurt my brother.
Laertes. I am satisfied in nature,
    Whose motive, in this case, should stir me most
    To my revenge: but in my terms of honour
    I stand aloof, and will no reconcilement,
    Till by some elder masters of known honour
    I have a voice and precedent of peace,
    To keep my name ungored. But till that time
    I do receive your offer'd love like love
    And will not wrong it.
Hamlet. I embrace it freely,
    And will this brother's wager frankly play.
    Give us the foils. Come on.
Laertes. Come, one for me.
Hamlet. I'll be your foil, Laertes: in mine ignorance
    Your skill shall, like a star i' the darkest night,
    Stick fiery off indeed.
Laertes. You mock me, sir.
Hamlet. No, by this hand.

King. Give them the foils, young Osric. Cousin Hamlet,
  You know the wager?
Hamlet. Very well, my lord;
  Your grace has laid the odds o' the weaker side.
King. I do not fear it; I have seen you both:
  But since he is better'd, we have therefore odds.
Laertes. This is too heavy; let me see another.
      Hamlet. This likes me well. These foils have all a length?

[*They prepare to play.*

Osric. Ay, my good lord.
King. Set me the stoups of wine upon that table.
  If Hamlet give the first or second hit,
  Or quit in answer of the third exchange,
  Let all the battlements their ordnance fire;
  The king shall drink to Hamlet's better breath;
  And in the cup an union shall he throw,
  Richer than that which four successive kings
  In Denmark's crown have worn. Give me the cups;
  And let the kettle to the trumpet speak,
  The trumpet to the cannoneer without,
  The cannons to the heavens, the heaven to earth,
  'Now the king drinks to Hamlet.' Come, begin;
  And you, the judges, bear a wary eye.
Hamlet. Come on, sir.
Laertes. Come, my lord. [*They play.*
Hamlet. One.
Laertes. No.
Hamlet. Judgement.
Osric. A hit, a very palpable hit.
Laertes. Well; again.
King. Stay; give me drink. Hamlet, this pearl is thine;
  Here's to thy health.

[*Trumpets sound, and cannon shot off within.*

Give him the cup.
Hamlet. I'll play this bout first; set it by awhile. Come.
  [*They play.*]
  Another hit; what say you?

Laertes. A touch, a touch, I do confess.

King. Our son shall win.

Queen. He's fat and scant of breath.

    Here, Hamlet, take my napkin, rub thy brows:

    The queen carouses to thy fortune, Hamlet.

Hamlet. Good madam!

King. Gertrude, do not drink.

Queen. I will, my lord; I pray you, pardon me.

King. [*Aside*] It is the poison'd cup; it is too late.

Hamlet. I dare not drink yet, madam; by and by.

Queen. Come, let me wipe thy face.

Laertes. My lord, I'll hit him now.

King. I do not think't.

Laertes. [*Aside*] And yet it is almost against my conscience.

Hamlet. Come, for the third, Laertes: you but dally;

    I pray you, pass with your best violence;

    I am afeard you make a wanton of me.

Laertes. Say you so? come on. [*They play.*

Osric. Nothing, neither way.

Laertes. Have at you now!

    [*Laertes wounds Hamlet; then, in scuffling, they change
       rapiers, and Hamlet wounds Laertes.*

King. Part them; they are incensed.

Hamlet. Nay, come, again. [*The Queen falls.*

Osric. Look to the queen there, ho!

Horatio. They bleed on both sides. How is it, my lord?

Osric. How is't, Laertes?

Laertes. Why, as a woodcock to mine own springe, Osric;

    I am justly kill'd with mine own treachery.

Hamlet. How does the queen?

King. She swounds to see them bleed.

Queen. No, no, the drink, the drink, – O my dear Hamlet, –

    The drink, the drink! I am poison'd. [*Dies.*

Hamlet. O villany! Ho! let the door be lock'd:

    Treachery! seek it out.

Laertes. It is here, Hamlet: Hamlet, thou art slain;

    No medicine in the world can do thee good,

    In thee there is not half an hour of life;

    The treacherous instrument is in thy hand,

Unbated and envenom'd: the foul practice
Hath turn'd itself on me; lo, here I lie,
Never to rise again: thy mother's poison'd:
I can no more: the king, the king's to blame.
Hamlet. The point envenom'd too!
    Then, venom, to thy work.

[*Stabs the King.*

All. Treason! treason!
King. O, yet defend me, friends; I am but hurt.
Hamlet. Here, thou incestuous, murderous, damned Dane,
    Drink off this potion: is thy union here?
    Follow my mother.

[*King dies.*

Laertes. He is justly served;
    It is a poison temper'd by himself.
    Exchange forgiveness with me, noble Hamlet:
    Mine and my father's death come not upon thee,
    Nor thine on me!

[*Dies.*

Hamlet. Heaven make thee free of it! I follow thee.
    I am dead, Horatio. Wretched queen, adieu!
    You that look pale and tremble at this chance,
    That are but mutes or audience to this act,
    Had I but time – as this fell sergeant, death,
    Is strict in his arrest – O, I could tell you –
    But let it be. Horatio, I am dead;
    Thou livest; report me and my cause aright
    To the unsatisfied.
Horatio. Never believe it:
    I am more an antique Roman than a Dane:
    Here's yet some liquor left.
Hamlet. As thou'rt a man,
    Give me the cup: let go; by heaven, I'll have't.
    O good Horatio, what a wounded name,
    Things standing thus unknown, shall live behind me!

If thou didst ever hold me in thy heart,
Absent thee from felicity awhile,
And in this harsh world draw thy breath in pain,
To tell my story.

[*March afar off, and shot within.*

What warlike noise is this?
Osric. Young Fortinbras, with conquest come from Poland,
To the ambassadors of England gives
This warlike volley.
Hamlet. O, I die, Horatio;
The potent poison quite o'er-crows my spirit:
I cannot live to hear the news from England;
But I do prophesy the election lights
On Fortinbras: he has my dying voice;
So tell him, with the occurrents, more and less,
Which have solicited. The rest is silence.

[*Dies.*

Horatio. Now cracks a noble heart. Good night, sweet prince,
And flights of angels sing thee to thy rest!
Why does the drum come hither?

[*March within.*

Enter Fortinbras, *and the* English Ambassadors,
with drum, colours, and Attendants.

Fortinbras. Where is this sight?
Horatio. What is it you would see?
If aught of woe or wonder, cease your search.
Fortinbras. This quarry cries on havoc. O proud death,
What feast is toward in thine eternal cell,
That thou so many princes at a shot
So bloodily hast struck?
First Amb. The sight is dismal;
And our affairs from England come too late:
The ears are senseless that should give us hearing.
To tell him his commandment is fulfill'd,

That Rosencrantz and Guildenstern are dead:
Where should we have our thanks?
Horatio. Not from his mouth
  Had it the ability of life to thank you:
  He never gave commandment for their death.
  But since, so jump upon this bloody question,
  You from the Polack wars, and you from England,
  Are here arrived, give order that these bodies
  High on a stage be placed to the view;
  And let me speak to the yet unknowing world
  How these things came about: so shall you hear
  Of carnal, bloody and unnatural acts,
  Of accidental judgements, casual slaughters,
  Of deaths put on by cunning and forced cause,
  And, in this upshot, purposes mistook
  Fall'n on the inventors' heads: all this can I
  Truly deliver.
Fortinbras. Let us haste to hear it,
  And call the noblest to the audience.
  For me, with sorrow I embrace my fortune:
  I have some rights of memory in this kingdom,
  Which now to claim my vantage doth invite me.
Horatio. Of that I shall have also cause to speak,
  And from his mouth whose voice will draw on more:
  But let this same be presently perform'd,
  Even while men's minds are wild; lest more mischance
  On plots and errors happen.
Fortinbras. Let four captains
  Bear Hamlet, like a soldier, to the stage;
  For he was likely, had he been put on,
  To have proved most royally: and, for his passage,
  The soldiers' music and the rites of war
  Speak loudly for him.
  Take up the bodies: such a sight as this
  Becomes the field, but here shows much amiss.
  Go, bid the soldiers shoot.

> [*A dead march. Exeunt, bearing off the bodies:
> after which a peal of ordnance is shot off.*

MACBETH

CONTENTS

DRAMATIS PERSONÆ

Duncan, King of Scotland.
Malcolm, his Son.
Donalbain, his Son.
Macbeth, General in the King's Army.
Banquo, General in the King's Army.
Macduff, Nobleman of Scotland.
Lennox, Nobleman of Scotland.
Ross, Nobleman of Scotland.
Menteith, Nobleman of Scotland.
Angus, Nobleman of Scotland.
Caithness, Nobleman of Scotland.
Fleance, Son to Banquo.
Siward, Earl of Northumberland, General of the English Forces.
Young Siward, his Son.
Seyton, an Officer attending on Macbeth.
Boy, Son to Macduff.
An English Doctor. A Scotch Doctor. A Soldier. A Porter. An Old Man.

Lady Macbeth.
Lady Macduff. Gentlewoman attending on Lady Macbeth.
Hecate, and three Witches.

Lords, Gentlemen, Officers, Soldiers, Murderers, Attendants, and Messengers.

The Ghost of Banquo and several other Apparitions.

Scene: In the end of the Fourth Act, in England; through the rest of the Play, in Scotland; and chiefly at Macbeth's Castle.

Act I.

An open Place. Thunder and Lightning.

[*Enter three* Witches.]

First Witch. When shall we three meet again?
   In thunder, lightning, or in rain?
Second Witch. When the hurlyburly's done,
   When the battle's lost and won.
Third Witch. That will be ere the set of sun.
First Witch. Where the place?
Second Witch. Upon the heath.
Third Witch. There to meet with *Macbeth.*
First Witch. I come, Graymalkin!
All. Paddock calls: – anon: –
   Fair is foul, and foul is fair:
   Hover through the fog and filthy air.

[Witches *vanish.*]

SCENE TWO

A Camp near Forres.

[*Alarum within. Enter* King Duncan, Malcolm, Donalbain,
Lennox, *with* Attendants, *meeting a bleeding* Soldier.]

Duncan. What bloody man is that? He can report,
    As seemeth by his plight, of the revolt
    The newest state.
Malcolm. This is the sergeant
    Who, like a good and hardy soldier, fought
    'Gainst my captivity. – Hail, brave friend!
    Say to the king the knowledge of the broil
    As thou didst leave it.
Soldier. Doubtful it stood;
    As two spent swimmers that do cling together
    And choke their art. The merciless Macdonwald, –
    Worthy to be a rebel, – for to that
    The multiplying villainies of nature
    Do swarm upon him, – from the Western isles
    Of kerns and gallowglasses is supplied;
    And fortune, on his damned quarrel smiling,
    Show'd like a rebel's whore. But all's too weak;
    For brave Macbeth, – well he deserves that name, –
    Disdaining fortune, with his brandish'd steel,
    Which smok'd with bloody execution,
    Like valor's minion,
    Carv'd out his passag tTill he fac'd the slave;
    And ne'er shook hands, nor bade farewell to him,

Till he unseam'd him from the nave to the chaps,
And fix'd his head upon our battlements.
Duncan. O valiant cousin! worthy gentleman!
Soldier. As whence the sun 'gins his reflection
    Shipwrecking storms and direful thunders break;
    So from that spring, whence comfort seem'd to come
    Discomfort swells. Mark, King of Scotland, mark:
    No sooner justice had, with valor arm'd,
    Compell'd these skipping kerns to trust their heels,
    But the Norweyan lord, surveying vantage,
    With furbish'd arms and new supplies of men,
    Began a fresh assault.
Duncan. Dismay'd not this
    Our captains, Macbeth and Banquo?
Soldier. Yes;
    As sparrows eagles, or the hare the lion.
    If I say sooth, I must report they were
    As cannons overcharg'd with double cracks;
    So they
    Doubly redoubled strokes upon the foe:
    Except they meant to bathe in reeking wounds,
    Or memorize another Golgotha,
    I cannot tell: –
    But I am faint; my gashes cry for help.
Duncan. So well thy words become thee as thy wounds;
    They smack of honor both. – Go, get him surgeons.

[*Exit* Soldier, *attended.*]

Who comes here?
Malcolm. The worthy Thane of Ross.
Lennox. What a haste looks through his eyes! So should he look
    That seems to speak things strange.

[*Enter* Ross.]

Ross. God save the King!
Duncan. Whence cam'st thou, worthy thane?
Ross. From Fife, great king;
    Where the Norweyan banners flout the sky
    And fan our people cold.

Norway himself, with terrible numbers,
Assisted by that most disloyal traitor
The Thane of Cawdor, began a dismal conflict;
Till that Bellona's bridegroom, lapp'd in proof,
Confronted him with self-comparisons,
Point against point rebellious, arm 'gainst arm,
Curbing his lavish spirit: and, to conclude,
The victory fell on us.

Duncan. Great happiness!

Ross. That now
Sweno, the Norways' king, craves composition;
Nor would we deign him burial of his men
Till he disbursed, at Saint Colme's-inch,
Ten thousand dollars to our general use.

Duncan. No more that Thane of Cawdor shall deceive
Our bosom interest: – go pronounce his present death,
And with his former title greet Macbeth.

Ross. I'll see it done.

Duncan. What he hath lost, noble Macbeth hath won.

[*Exeunt.*]

SCENE THREE

A heath.

[*Thunder. Enter the three* Witches.]

First Witch. Where hast thou been, sister?
Second Witch. Killing swine.
Third Witch. Sister, where thou?
First Witch. A sailor's wife had chestnuts in her lap,
    And mounch'd, and mounch'd, and mounch'd: – "Give me," quoth I:
    "Aroint thee, witch!" the rump-fed ronyon cries.
    Her husband's to Aleppo gone, master o' the Tiger:
    But in a sieve I'll thither sail,
    And, like a rat without a tail,
    I'll do, I'll do, and I'll do.
Second Witch. I'll give thee a wind.
First Witch. Thou art kind.
Third Witch. And I another.
First Witch. I myself have all the other:
    And the very ports they blow,
    All the quarters that they know
    I' the shipman's card.
    I will drain him dry as hay:
    Sleep shall neither night nor day
    Hang upon his pent-house lid;
    He shall live a man forbid:
    Weary seven-nights nine times nine
    Shall he dwindle, peak, and pine:
    Though his bark cannot be lost,

Yet it shall be tempest-tost. –
Look what I have.
Second Witch. Show me, show me.
First Witch. Here I have a pilot's thumb,
Wreck'd as homeward he did come.

[*Drum within.*]

Third Witch. A drum, a drum!
Macbeth doth come.
All. The weird sisters, hand in hand,
Posters of the sea and land,
Thus do go about, about:
Thrice to thine, and thrice to mine,
And thrice again, to make up nine: –
Peace! – the charm's wound up.

[*Enter* Macbeth *and* Banquo.]

Macbeth. So foul and fair a day I have not seen.
Banquo. How far is't call'd to Forres? – What are these
So wither'd, and so wild in their attire,
That look not like the inhabitants o' the earth,
And yet are on't? – Live you? or are you aught
That man may question? You seem to understand me,
By each at once her chappy finger laying
Upon her skinny lips: – you should be women,
And yet your beards forbid me to interpret
That you are so.
Macbeth. Speak, if you can; – what are you?
First Witch. All hail, Macbeth! hail to thee, Thane of Glamis!
Second Witch. All hail, Macbeth! hail to thee, Thane of Cawdor!
Third Witch. All hail, Macbeth! that shalt be king hereafter!
Banquo. Good sir, why do you start; and seem to fear
Things that do sound so fair? – I' the name of truth,
Are ye fantastical, or that indeed
Which outwardly ye show? My noble partner
You greet with present grace and great prediction
Of noble having and of royal hope,
That he seems rapt withal: – to me you speak not:
If you can look into the seeds of time,

And say which grain will grow, and which will not,
Speak then to me, who neither beg nor fear
Your favors nor your hate.
First Witch. Hail!
Second Witch. Hail!
Third Witch. Hail!
First Witch. Lesser than Macbeth, and greater.
Second Witch. Not so happy, yet much happier.
Third Witch. Thou shalt get kings, though thou be none:
    So all hail, Macbeth and Banquo!
First Witch. Banquo and Macbeth, all hail!
Macbeth. Stay, you imperfect speakers, tell me more:
    By Sinel's death I know I am Thane of Glamis;
    But how of Cawdor? The Thane of Cawdor lives,
    A prosperous gentleman; and to be king
    Stands not within the prospect of belief,
    No more than to be Cawdor. Say from whence
    You owe this strange intelligence? or why
    Upon this blasted heath you stop our way
    With such prophetic greeting? – Speak, I charge you.

[Witches *vanish*.]

Banquo. The earth hath bubbles, as the water has,
    And these are of them: – whither are they vanish'd?
Macbeth. Into the air; and what seem'd corporal melted
    As breath into the wind. – Would they had stay'd!
Banquo. Were such things here as we do speak about?
    Or have we eaten on the insane root
    That takes the reason prisoner?
Macbeth. Your children shall be kings.
Banquo. You shall be king.
Macbeth. And Thane of Cawdor too; went it not so?
Banquo. To the selfsame tune and words. Who's here?

[*Enter* Ross *and* Angus.]

Ross. The king hath happily receiv'd, Macbeth,
    The news of thy success: and when he reads
    Thy personal venture in the rebels' fight,
    His wonders and his praises do contend

Which should be thine or his: silenc'd with that,
In viewing o'er the rest o' the self-same day,
He finds thee in the stout Norweyan ranks,
Nothing afeard of what thyself didst make,
Strange images of death. As thick as hail
Came post with post; and every one did bear
Thy praises in his kingdom's great defense,
And pour'd them down before him.
Angus. We are sent
To give thee, from our royal master, thanks;
Only to herald thee into his sight,
Not pay thee.
Ross. And, for an earnest of a greater honor,
He bade me, from him, call thee Thane of Cawdor:
In which addition, hail, most worthy thane,
For it is thine.
Banquo. What, can the devil speak true?
Macbeth. The Thane of Cawdor lives: why do you dress me
In borrow'd robes?
Angus. Who was the Thane lives yet;
But under heavy judgement bears that life
Which he deserves to lose. Whether he was combin'd
With those of Norway, or did line the rebel
With hidden help and vantage, or that with both
He labour'd in his country's wreck, I know not;
But treasons capital, confess'd and proved,
Have overthrown him.
Macbeth. [*Aside.*]
Glamis, and Thane of Cawdor:
The greatest is behind. – Thanks for your pains. –
Do you not hope your children shall be kings,
When those that gave the Thane of Cawdor to me
Promis'd no less to them?
Banquo. That, trusted home,
Might yet enkindle you unto the crown,
Besides the Thane of Cawdor. But 'tis strange:
And oftentimes to win us to our harm,
The instruments of darkness tell us truths;
Win us with honest trifles, to betray's
In deepest consequence. –
Cousins, a word, I pray you.

Macbeth. [*Aside.*]
    Two truths are told,
    As happy prologues to the swelling act
    Of the imperial theme. – I thank you, gentlemen. –
    [*Aside.*]
    This supernatural soliciting
    Cannot be ill; cannot be good: – if ill,
    Why hath it given me earnest of success,
    Commencing in a truth? I am Thane of Cawdor:
    If good, why do I yield to that suggestion
    Whose horrid image doth unfix my hair,
    And make my seated heart knock at my ribs,
    Against the use of nature? Present fears
    Are less than horrible imaginings:
    My thought, whose murder yet is but fantastical,
    Shakes so my single state of man, that function
    Is smother'd in surmise; and nothing is
    But what is not.
Banquo. Look, how our partner's rapt.
Macbeth. [*Aside.*]
    If chance will have me king, why, chance may crown me
    Without my stir.
Banquo. New honors come upon him,
    Like our strange garments, cleave not to their mould
    But with the aid of use.
Macbeth. [*Aside.*]
    Come what come may,
    Time and the hour runs through the roughest day.
Banquo. Worthy Macbeth, we stay upon your leisure.
Macbeth. Give me your favor: – my dull brain was wrought
    With things forgotten. Kind gentlemen, your pains
    Are register'd where every day I turn
    The leaf to read them. – Let us toward the king. –
    Think upon what hath chanc'd; and, at more time,
    The interim having weigh'd it, let us speak
    Our free hearts each to other.
Banquo. Very gladly.
Macbeth. Till then, enough. – Come, friends.

[*Exeunt.*]

SCENE FOUR

Forres. A Room in the Palace.

[*Flourish. Enter* Duncan, Malcolm, Donalbain, Lennox, *and* Attendants.]

Duncan. Is execution done on Cawdor? Are not
    Those in commission yet return'd?
Malcolm. My liege,
    They are not yet come back. But I have spoke
    With one that saw him die: who did report,
    That very frankly he confess'd his treasons;
    Implor'd your highness' pardon; and set forth
    A deep repentance: nothing in his life
    Became him like the leaving it; he died
    As one that had been studied in his death,
    To throw away the dearest thing he ow'd
    As 'twere a careless trifle.
Duncan. There's no art
    To find the mind's construction in the face:
    He was a gentleman on whom I built
    An absolute trust. –

[*Enter* Macbeth, Banquo, Ross, *and* Angus.]

O worthiest cousin!
The sin of my ingratitude even now
Was heavy on me: thou art so far before,
That swiftest wing of recompense is slow
To overtake thee. Would thou hadst less deserv'd;
That the proportion both of thanks and payment

Might have been mine! only I have left to say,
More is thy due than more than all can pay.
Macbeth. The service and the loyalty I owe,
In doing it, pays itself. Your highness' part
Is to receive our duties: and our duties
Are to your throne and state, children and servants;
Which do but what they should, by doing everything
Safe toward your love and honor.
Duncan. Welcome hither:
I have begun to plant thee, and will labor
To make thee full of growing. – Noble Banquo,
That hast no less deserv'd, nor must be known
No less to have done so,let me infold thee
And hold thee to my heart.
Banquo. There if I grow,
The harvest is your own.
Duncan. My plenteous joys,
Wanton in fulness, seek to hide themselves
In drops of sorrow. – Sons, kinsmen, thanes,
And you whose places are the nearest, know,
We will establish our estate upon
Our eldest, Malcolm; whom we name hereafter
The Prince of Cumberland: which honor must
Not unaccompanied invest him only,
But signs of nobleness, like stars, shall shine
On all deservers. – From hence to Inverness,
And bind us further to you.
Macbeth. The rest is labor, which is not us'd for you:
I'll be myself the harbinger, and make joyful
The hearing of my wife with your approach;
So, humbly take my leave.
Duncan. My worthy Cawdor!
Macbeth. [*Aside.*]
The Prince of Cumberland! – That is a step,
On which I must fall down, or else o'erleap,
For in my way it lies. Stars, hide your fires!
Let not light see my black and deep desires:
The eye wink at the hand! yet let that be,
Which the eye fears, when it is done, to see.

[*Exit.*]

Duncan. True, worthy Banquo! – he is full so valiant;
  And in his commendations I am fed, –
  It is a banquet to me. Let us after him,
  Whose care is gone before to bid us welcome:
  It is a peerless kinsman.

  [*Flourish. Exeunt.*]

SCENE FIVE

Inverness. A Room in Macbeth's *Castle.*

[*Enter* Lady Macbeth, *reading a letter.*]

Lady Macbeth. "They met me in the day of success; and I have
learned by the perfectest report they have more in them than mortal knowledge. When I burned in desire to question them further,
they made themselves air, into which they vanished. Whiles I stood
rapt in the wonder of it, came missives from the king, who all-
hailed me, 'Thane of Cawdor'; by which title, before, these weird
sisters saluted me, and referred me to the coming on of time, with
'Hail, king that shalt be!' This have I thought good to deliver thee,
my dearest partner of greatness; that thou mightst not lose the dues
of rejoicing, by being ignorant of what greatness is promised thee.
Lay it to thy heart, and farewell."
Glamis thou art, and Cawdor; and shalt be
What thou art promis'd; yet do I fear thy nature;
It is too full o' the milk of human kindness
To catch the nearest way: thou wouldst be great;
Art not without ambition; but without
The illness should attend it. What thou wouldst highly,
That wouldst thou holily; wouldst not play false,
And yet wouldst wrongly win: thou'dst have, great Glamis,
That which cries, "Thus thou must do, if thou have it:
And that which rather thou dost fear to do
Than wishest should be undone." Hie thee hither,
That I may pour my spirits in thine ear;
And chastise with the valor of my tongue
All that impedes thee from the golden round,

Which fate and metaphysical aid doth seem
To have thee crown'd withal.

[*Enter an* Attendant.]

What is your tidings?
Attendant. The king comes here tonight.
Lady Macbeth. Thou'rt mad to say it:
    Is not thy master with him? who, were't so,
    Would have inform'd for preparation.
Attendant. So please you, it is true: – our thane is coming:
    One of my fellows had the speed of him;
    Who, almost dead for breath, had scarcely more
    Than would make up his message.
Lady Macbeth. Give him tending;
    He brings great news.

[*Exit* Attendant.]

The raven himself is hoarse
That croaks the fatal entrance of Duncan
Under my battlements. Come, you spirits
That tend on mortal thoughts, unsex me here;
And fill me, from the crown to the toe, top-full
Of direst cruelty! make thick my blood,
Stop up the access and passage to remorse,
That no compunctious visitings of nature
Shake my fell purpose, nor keep peace between
The effect and it! Come to my woman's breasts,
And take my milk for gall, your murdering ministers,
Wherever in your sightless substances
You wait on nature's mischief! Come, thick night,
And pall thee in the dunnest smoke of hell
That my keen knife see not the wound it makes
Nor heaven peep through the blanket of the dark
To cry, "Hold, hold!"

[*Enter* Macbeth.]

Great Glamis! Worthy Cawdor!
Greater than both, by the all-hail hereafter!

Thy letters have transported me beyond
This ignorant present, and I feel now
The future in the instant.
Macbeth. My dearest love,
   Duncan comes here tonight.
Lady Macbeth. And when goes hence?
Macbeth. To-morrow, – as he purposes.
Lady Macbeth. O, never
   Shall sun that morrow see!
   Your face, my thane, is as a book where men
   May read strange matters: – to beguile the time,
   Look like the time; bear welcome in your eye,
   Your hand, your tongue: look like the innocent flower,
   But be the serpent under't. He that's coming
   Must be provided for: and you shall put
   This night's great business into my despatch;
   Which shall to all our nights and days to come
   Give solely sovereign sway and masterdom.
Macbeth. We will speak further.
Lady Macbeth. Only look up clear;
   To alter favor ever is to fear:
   Leave all the rest to me.

[Exeunt.]

SCENE SIX

The same. Before the Castle.

[*Hautboys*. Servants *of* Macbeth *attending.*]
[*Enter* Duncan, Malcolm, Donalbain, Banquo, Lennox, Macduff, Ross, Angus, *and* Attendants.]

Duncan. This castle hath a pleasant seat: the air
  Nimbly and sweetly recommends itself
  Unto our gentle senses.
Banquo. This guest of summer,
  The temple-haunting martlet, does approve
  By his lov'd mansionry, that the heaven's breath
  Smells wooingly here: no jutty, frieze, buttress,
  Nor coigne of vantage, but this bird hath made
  His pendant bed and procreant cradle:
  Where they most breed and haunt, I have observ'd
  The air is delicate.

[*Enter* Lady Macbeth.]

Duncan. See, see, our honour'd hostess! –
  The love that follows us sometime is our trouble,
  Which still we thank as love. Herein I teach you
  How you shall bid God ild us for your pains,
  And thank us for your trouble.
Lady Macbeth. All our service
  In every point twice done, and then done double,
  Were poor and single business to contend
  Against those honours deep and broad wherewith

Your majesty loads our house: for those of old,
And the late dignities heap'd up to them,
We rest your hermits.
Duncan. Where's the Thane of Cawdor?
We cours'd him at the heels, and had a purpose
To be his purveyor: but he rides well;
And his great love, sharp as his spur, hath holp him
To his home before us. Fair and noble hostess,
We are your guest tonight.
Lady Macbeth. Your servants ever
Have theirs, themselves, and what is theirs, in compt,
To make their audit at your highness' pleasure,
Still to return your own.
Duncan. Give me your hand;
Conduct me to mine host: we love him highly,
And shall continue our graces towards him.
By your leave, hostess.

[*Exeunt.*]

SCENE SEVEN

The same. A Lobby in the Castle.

[*Hautboys and torches. Enter, and pass over, a* Sewer *and div-ers* Servants *with dishes and service. Then enter* Macbeth.]

Macbeth. If it were done when 'tis done, then 'twere well
   It were done quickly. If the assassination
   Could trammel up the consequence, and catch,
   With his surcease, success; that but this blow
   Might be the be-all and the end-all – here,
   But here, upon this bank and shoal of time, –
   We'd jump the life to come. But in these cases
   We still have judgement here; that we but teach
   Bloody instructions, which being taught, return
   To plague the inventor: this even-handed justice
   Commends the ingredients of our poison'd chalice
   To our own lips. He's here in double trust:
   First, as I am his kinsman and his subject,
   Strong both against the deed: then, as his host,
   Who should against his murderer shut the door,
   Not bear the knife myself. Besides, this Duncan
   Hath borne his faculties so meek, hath been
   So clear in his great office, that his virtues
   Will plead like angels, trumpet-tongued, against
   The deep damnation of his taking-off:
   And pity, like a naked new-born babe,
   Striding the blast, or heaven's cherubin, hors'd
   Upon the sightless couriers of the air,
   Shall blow the horrid deed in every eye,

That tears shall drown the wind. – I have no spur
To prick the sides of my intent, but only
Vaulting ambition, which o'erleaps itself,
And falls on the other.

[*Enter* Lady Macbeth.]

How now! what news?
Lady Macbeth. He has almost supp'd: why have you left the chamber?
Macbeth. Hath he ask'd for me?
Lady Macbeth. Know you not he has?
Macbeth. We will proceed no further in this business:
He hath honour'd me of late; and I have bought
Golden opinions from all sorts of people,
Which would be worn now in their newest gloss,
Not cast aside so soon.
Lady Macbeth. Was the hope drunk
Wherein you dress'd yourself? hath it slept since?
And wakes it now, to look so green and pale
At what it did so freely? From this time
Such I account thy love. Art thou afeard
To be the same in thine own act and valor
As thou art in desire? Wouldst thou have that
Which thou esteem'st the ornament of life,
And live a coward in thine own esteem;
Letting "I dare not" wait upon "I would,"
Like the poor cat i' the adage?
Macbeth. Pr'ythee, peace!
I dare do all that may become a man;
Who dares do more is none.
Lady Macbeth. What beast was't, then,
That made you break this enterprise to me?
When you durst do it, then you were a man;
And, to be more than what you were, you would
Be so much more the man. Nor time nor place
Did then adhere, and yet you would make both:
They have made themselves, and that their fitness now
Does unmake you. I have given suck, and know
How tender 'tis to love the babe that milks me:
I would, while it was smiling in my face,
Have pluck'd my nipple from his boneless gums

And dash'd the brains out, had I so sworn as you
Have done to this.
Macbeth. If we should fail?
Lady Macbeth. We fail!
　　But screw your courage to the sticking-place,
　　And we'll not fail. When Duncan is asleep, –
　　Whereto the rather shall his day's hard journey
　　Soundly invite him, his two chamberlains
　　Will I with wine and wassail so convince
　　That memory, the warder of the brain,
　　Shall be a fume, and the receipt of reason
　　A limbec only: when in swinish sleep
　　Their drenched natures lie as in a death,
　　What cannot you and I perform upon
　　The unguarded Duncan? what not put upon
　　His spongy officers; who shall bear the guilt
　　Of our great quell?
Macbeth. Bring forth men-children only;
　　For thy undaunted mettle should compose
　　Nothing but males. Will it not be receiv'd,
　　When we have mark'd with blood those sleepy two
　　Of his own chamber, and us'd their very daggers,
　　That they have don't?
Lady Macbeth. Who dares receive it other,
　　As we shall make our griefs and clamor roar
　　Upon his death?
Macbeth. I am settled, and bend up
　　Each corporal agent to this terrible feat.
　　Away, and mock the time with fairest show:
　　False face must hide what the false heart doth know.

[*Exeunt.*]

Act II.

SCENE ONE

Inverness. Court within the Castle.

[*Enter* Banquo, *preceded by* Fleance *with a torch.*]

Banquo. How goes the night, boy?
Fleance. The moon is down; I have not heard the clock.
Banquo. And she goes down at twelve.
Fleance. I take't, 'tis later, sir.
Banquo. Hold, take my sword. – There's husbandry in heaven;
    Their candles are all out: – take thee that too. –
    A heavy summons lies like lead upon me,
    And yet I would not sleep: – merciful powers,
    Restrain in me the cursed thoughts that nature
    Gives way to in repose! – Give me my sword.
    Who's there?

[*Enter* Macbeth, *and a* Servant *with a torch.*]

Macbeth. A friend.
Banquo. What, sir, not yet at rest? The king's a-bed:
    He hath been in unusual pleasure and
    Sent forth great largess to your officers:
    This diamond he greets your wife withal,
    By the name of most kind hostess; and shut up
    In measureless content.
Macbeth. Being unprepar'd,
    Our will became the servant to defect;
    Which else should free have wrought.

Banquo. All's well.
  I dreamt last night of the three weird sisters:
  To you they have show'd some truth.
Macbeth. I think not of them:
  Yet, when we can entreat an hour to serve,
  We would spend it in some words upon that business,
  If you would grant the time.
Banquo. At your kind'st leisure.
Macbeth. If you shall cleave to my consent, – when 'tis,
  It shall make honor for you.
Banquo. So I lose none
  In seeking to augment it, but still keep
  My bosom franchis'd, and allegiance clear,
  I shall be counsell'd.
Macbeth. Good repose the while!
Banquo. Thanks, sir: the like to you!

[*Exeunt* Banquo *and* Fleance.]

Macbeth. Go bid thy mistress, when my drink is ready,
  She strike upon the bell. Get thee to bed.

[*Exit* Servant.]

Is this a dagger which I see before me,
The handle toward my hand? Come, let me clutch thee: –
I have thee not, and yet I see thee still.
Art thou not, fatal vision, sensible
To feeling as to sight? or art thou but
A dagger of the mind, a false creation,
Proceeding from the heat-oppressed brain?
I see thee yet, in form as palpable
As this which now I draw.
Thou marshall'st me the way that I was going;
And such an instrument I was to use.
Mine eyes are made the fools o' the other senses,
Or else worth all the rest: I see thee still;
And on thy blade and dudgeon gouts of blood,
Which was not so before. – There's no such thing:
It is the bloody business which informs
Thus to mine eyes. – Now o'er the one half-world

Nature seems dead, and wicked dreams abuse
The curtain'd sleep; now witchcraft celebrates
Pale Hecate's offerings; and wither'd murder,
Alarum'd by his sentinel, the wolf,
Whose howl's his watch, thus with his stealthy pace,
With Tarquin's ravishing strides, towards his design
Moves like a ghost. – Thou sure and firm-set earth,
Hear not my steps, which way they walk, for fear
Thy very stones prate of my whereabout,
And take the present horror from the time,
Which now suits with it. – Whiles I threat, he lives;
Words to the heat of deeds too cold breath gives.

[*A bell rings.*]

I go, and it is done; the bell invites me.
Hear it not, Duncan, for it is a knell
That summons thee to heaven or to hell.

[*Exit.*]

[*Enter* Lady Macbeth.]

Lady Macbeth. That which hath made them drunk hath made me bold:
  What hath quench'd them hath given me fire. – Hark! – Peace!
  It was the owl that shriek'd, the fatal bellman,
  Which gives the stern'st good night. He is about it:
  The doors are open; and the surfeited grooms
  Do mock their charge with snores: I have drugg'd their possets
  That death and nature do contend about them,
  Whether they live or die.
Macbeth. [*Within.*]
  Who's there? – what, ho!
Lady Macbeth. Alack! I am afraid they have awak'd,
  And 'tis not done: the attempt, and not the deed,
  Confounds us. – Hark! – I laid their daggers ready;
  He could not miss 'em. – Had he not resembled
  My father as he slept, I had done't. – My husband!

[*Re-enter* Macbeth.]

Macbeth. I have done the deed. – Didst thou not hear a noise?
Lady Macbeth. I heard the owl scream and the crickets cry.
    Did not you speak?
Macbeth. When?
Lady Macbeth. Now.
Macbeth. As I descended?
Lady Macbeth. Ay.
Macbeth. Hark! –
    Who lies i' the second chamber?
Lady Macbeth. Donalbain.
Macbeth. This is a sorry sight.

[*Looking on his hands.*]

Lady Macbeth. A foolish thought, to say a sorry sight.
Macbeth. There's one did laugh in's sleep, and one cried, "Murder!"
    That they did wake each other: I stood and heard them:
    But they did say their prayers, and address'd them
    Again to sleep.
Lady Macbeth. There are two lodg'd together.
Macbeth. One cried, "God bless us!" and, "Amen," the other;
    As they had seen me with these hangman's hands.
    Listening their fear, I could not say "Amen,"
    When they did say, "God bless us."
Lady Macbeth. Consider it not so deeply.
Macbeth. But wherefore could not I pronounce "Amen"?
    I had most need of blessing, and "Amen"
    Stuck in my throat.
Lady Macbeth. These deeds must not be thought
    After these ways; so, it will make us mad.
Macbeth. I heard a voice cry, "Sleep no more!
    Macbeth does murder sleep," – the innocent sleep;
    Sleep that knits up the ravell'd sleave of care,
    The death of each day's life, sore labour's bath,
    Balm of hurt minds, great nature's second course,
    Chief nourisher in life's feast.
Lady Macbeth. What do you mean?
Macbeth. Still it cried, "Sleep no more!" to all the house:
    "Glamis hath murder'd sleep, and therefore Cawdor
    Shall sleep no more, – Macbeth shall sleep no more!"
Lady Macbeth. Who was it that thus cried? Why, worthy thane,

You do unbend your noble strength to think
So brainsickly of things. – Go get some water,
And wash this filthy witness from your hand. –
Why did you bring these daggers from the place?
They must lie there: go carry them; and smear
The sleepy grooms with blood.
Macbeth. I'll go no more:
I am afraid to think what I have done;
Look on't again I dare not.
Lady Macbeth. Infirm of purpose!
Give me the daggers: the sleeping and the dead
Are but as pictures: 'tis the eye of childhood
That fears a painted devil. If he do bleed,
I'll gild the faces of the grooms withal,
For it must seem their guilt.

[*Exit. Knocking within.*]

Macbeth. Whence is that knocking?
How is't with me, when every noise appals me?
What hands are here? Ha, they pluck out mine eyes!
Will all great Neptune's ocean wash this blood
Clean from my hand? No; this my hand will rather
The multitudinous seas incarnadine,
Making the green one red.

[*Re-enter* Lady Macbeth.]

Lady Macbeth. My hands are of your color, but I shame
To wear a heart so white. [Knocking within.]
I hear knocking
At the south entry: – retire we to our chamber.
A little water clears us of this deed:
How easy is it then! Your constancy
Hath left you unattended. –
[Knocking within.]
Hark, more
knocking:
Get on your nightgown, lest occasion call us
And show us to be watchers: – be not lost
So poorly in your thoughts.

Macbeth. To know my deed, 'twere best not know myself.
   [Knocking within.]
   Wake Duncan with thy knocking! I would thou couldst!

[*Exeunt.*]

[*Enter a Porter. Knocking within.*]

Porter. Here's a knocking indeed! If a man were porter of hell-gate,
   he should have old turning the key. [Knocking.]
   Knock, knock, knock. Who's there, i' the name of Belzebub? Here's
   a farmer that hanged himself on the expectation of plenty: come
   in time; have napkins enow about you; here you'll sweat for't. –
   [Knocking.]
   Knock, knock! Who's there, in the other devil's name? Faith, here's
   an equivocator, that could swear in both the scales against either
   scale, who committed treason enough for God's sake, yet could not
   equivocate to heaven: O, come in, equivocator. [Knocking.]
   Knock, knock, knock! Who's there? Faith, here's an English tailor
   come hither, for stealing out of a French hose: come in, tailor; here
   you may roast your goose. – [Knocking.]
   Knock, knock: never at quiet! What are you? – But this
   place is too cold for hell. I'll devil-porter it no further: I had
   thought to have let in some of all professions, that go the
   primrose way to the everlasting bonfire. [Knocking.]
Anon, anon! I pray you, remember the porter.

[*Opens the gate.*]

[*Enter* Macduff *and* Lennox.]

Macduff. Was it so late, friend, ere you went to bed,
   That you do lie so late?
Porter. Faith, sir, we were carousing till the second cock: and drink,
   sir, is a great provoker of three things.
Macduff. What three things does drink especially provoke?
Porter. Marry, sir, nose-painting, sleep, and urine. Lechery, sir, it provokes and unprovokes; it provokes the desire, but it takes away the
   performance: therefore much drink may be said to be an equivocator with lechery: it makes him, and it mars him; it sets him on,
   and it takes him off; it persuades him, and disheartens him; makes

him stand to, and not stand to: in conclusion, equivocates him in a
sleep, and giving him the lie, leaves him.

Macduff. I believe drink gave thee the lie last night.

Porter. That it did, sir, i' the very throat o' me; but I requited him for
his lie; and, I think, being too strong for him, though he took up
my legs sometime, yet I made a shift to cast him.

Macduff. Is thy master stirring? –
Our knocking has awak'd him; here he comes.

[*Enter* Macbeth.]

Lennox. Good morrow, noble sir!

Macbeth. Good morrow, both!

Macduff. Is the king stirring, worthy thane?

Macbeth. Not yet.

Macduff. He did command me to call timely on him:
I have almost slipp'd the hour.

Macbeth. I'll bring you to him.

Macduff. I know this is a joyful trouble to you;
But yet 'tis one.

Macbeth. The labour we delight in physics pain.
This is the door.

Macduff. I'll make so bold to c*All*. For 'tis my limited service.

[*Exit* Macduff.]

Lennox. Goes the king hence to-day?

Macbeth. He does: he did appoint so.

Lennox. The night has been unruly: where we lay,
Our chimneys were blown down: and, as they say,
Lamentings heard i' the air, strange screams of death;
And prophesying, with accents terrible,
Of dire combustion and confus'd events,
New hatch'd to the woeful time: the obscure bird
Clamour'd the live-long night; some say the earth
Was feverous, and did shake.

Macbeth. 'Twas a rough night.

Lennox. My young remembrance cannot parallel
A fellow to it.

[*Re-enter* Macduff.]

Macduff. O horror, horror, horror! Tongue nor heart
    Cannot conceive nor name thee!
Macbeth, *Lennox.* What's the matter?
Macduff. Confusion now hath made his masterpiece!
    Most sacrilegious murder hath broke ope
    The Lord's anointed temple, and stole thence
    The life o' the building.
Macbeth. What is't you say? the life?
Lennox. Mean you his majesty?
Macduff. Approach the chamber, and destroy your sight
    With a new Gorgon: – do not bid me speak;
    See, and then speak yourselves.

[*Exeunt* Macbeth *and* Lennox.]

Awake, awake! –
Ring the alarum bell: – murder and treason!
Banquo and Donalbain! Malcolm! awake!
Shake off this downy sleep, death's counterfeit,
And look on death itself! up, up, and see
The great doom's image! Malcolm! Banquo!
As from your graves rise up, and walk like sprites
To countenance this horror!

[*Alarum-bell rings.*]

[*Re-enter* Lady Macbeth.]

Lady Macbeth. What's the business,
    That such a hideous trumpet calls to parley
    The sleepers of the house? speak, speak!
Macduff. O gentle lady,
    'Tis not for you to hear what I can speak:
    The repetition, in a woman's ear,
    Would murder as it fell.

[*Re-enter* Banquo.]

O Banquo, Banquo!
Our royal master's murder'd!

Lady Macbeth. Woe, alas!
   What, in our house?
Banquo. Too cruel any where. –
   Dear Duff, I pr'ythee, contradict thyself,
   And say it is not so.

        [*Re-enter* Macbeth and Lennox, with Ross.]

Macbeth. Had I but died an hour before this chance,
   I had liv'd a blessed time; for, from this instant
   There's nothing serious in mortality:
   All is but toys: renown and grace is dead;
   The wine of life is drawn, and the mere lees
   Is left this vault to brag of.

        [*Enter* Malcolm *and* Donalbain.]

Donalbain. What is amiss?
Macbeth. You are, and do not know't:
   The spring, the head, the fountain of your blood
   Is stopp'd; the very source of it is stopp'd.
Macduff. Your royal father's murder'd.
Malcolm. O, by whom?
Lennox. Those of his chamber, as it seem'd, had done't:
   Their hands and faces were all badg'd with blood;
   So were their daggers, which, unwip'd, we found
   Upon their pillows:
   They star'd, and were distracted; no man's life
   Was to be trusted with them.
Macbeth. O, yet I do repent me of my fury,
   That I did kill them.
Macduff. Wherefore did you so?
Macbeth. Who can be wise, amaz'd, temperate, and furious,
   Loyal and neutral, in a moment? No man:
   The expedition of my violent love
   Outrun the pauser reason. Here lay Duncan,
   His silver skin lac'd with his golden blood;
   And his gash'd stabs look'd like a breach in nature
   For ruin's wasteful entrance: there, the murderers,
   Steep'd in the colours of their trade, their daggers
   Unmannerly breech'd with gore: who could refrain,

  That had a heart to love, and in that heart
  Courage to make's love known?
Lady Macbeth. Help me hence, ho!
Macduff. Look to the lady.
Malcolm. Why do we hold our tongues,
  That most may claim this argument for ours?
Donalbain. What should be spoken here, where our fate,
  Hid in an auger hole, may rush, and seize us?
  Let's away;
  Our tears are not yet brew'd.
Malcolm. Nor our strong sorrow
  Upon the foot of motion.
Banquo. Look to the lady: –

    [*Lady Macbeth is carried out.*]

  And when we have our naked frailties hid,
  That suffer in exposure, let us meet,
  And question this most bloody piece of work
  To know it further. Fears and scruples shake us:
  In the great hand of God I stand; and thence,
  Against the undivulg'd pretense I fight
  Of treasonous malice.
Macduff. And so do I.
All. So all.
Macbeth. Let's briefly put on manly readiness,
  And meet i' the hall together.
All. Well contented.

  [*Exeunt all but* Malcolm *and* Donalbain.]

Malcolm. What will you do? Let's not consort with them:
  To show an unfelt sorrow is an office
  Which the false man does easy. I'll to England.
Donalbain. To Ireland, I; our separated fortune
  Shall keep us both the safer: where we are,
  There's daggers in men's smiles: the near in blood,
  The nearer bloody.
Malcolm. This murderous shaft that's shot
  Hath not yet lighted; and our safest way
  Is to avoid the aim. Therefore to horse;

And let us not be dainty of leave-taking,
But shift away: there's warrant in that theft
Which steals itself, when there's no mercy left.

[*Exeunt.*]

SCENE TWO

[*Enter* Ross *and an old* Man.]

Old Man. Threescore and ten I can remember well:
    Within the volume of which time I have seen
    Hours dreadful and things strange; but this sore night
    Hath trifled former knowings.
Ross. Ah, good father,
    Thou seest, the heavens, as troubled with man's act,
    Threaten his bloody stage: by the clock 'tis day,
    And yet dark night strangles the travelling lamp;
    Is't night's predominance, or the day's shame,
    That darkness does the face of earth entomb,
    When living light should kiss it?
Old Man. 'Tis unnatural,
    Even like the deed that's done. On Tuesday last,
    A falcon, towering in her pride of place,
    Was by a mousing owl hawk'd at and kill'd.
Ross. And Duncan's horses, – a thing most strange and certain, –
    Beauteous and swift, the minions of their race,
    Turn'd wild in nature, broke their stalls, flung out,
    Contending 'gainst obedience, as they would make
    War with mankind.
Old Man. 'Tis said they eat each other.
Ross. They did so; to the amazement of mine eyes,
    That look'd upon't.
    Here comes the good Macduff.

[Enter Macduff.]

How goes the world, sir, now?
Macduff. Why, see you not?
Ross. Is't known who did this more than bloody deed?
Macduff. Those that Macbeth hath slain.
Ross. Alas, the day!
  What good could they pretend?
. *Macduff.* They were suborn'd:
  Malcolm and Donalbain, the king's two sons,
  Are stol'n away and fled; which puts upon them
  Suspicion of the deed.
Ross. 'Gainst nature still:
  Thriftless ambition, that wilt ravin up
  Thine own life's means! – Then 'tis most like,
  The sovereignty will fall upon *Macbeth.*
Macduff. He is already nam'd; and gone to Scone
  To be invested.
Ross. Where is Duncan's body?
Macduff. Carried to Colme-kill,
  The sacred storehouse of his predecessors,
  And guardian of their bones.
Ross. Will you to Scone?
Macduff. No, cousin, I'll to Fife.
Ross. Well, I will thither.
Macduff. Well, may you see things well done there, – adieu! –
  Lest our old robes sit easier than our new!
Ross. Farewell, father.
Old Man. God's benison go with you; and with those
  That would make good of bad, and friends of foes!

[Exeunt.]

Act III.

SCENE ONE

Forres. A Room in the Palace.

[*Enter* Banquo.]

Banquo. Thou hast it now, – king, Cawdor, Glamis, all,
    As the weird women promis'd; and, I fear,
    Thou play'dst most foully for't; yet it was said
    It should not stand in thy posterity;
    But that myself should be the root and father
    Of many kings. If there come truth from them, –
    As upon thee, Macbeth, their speeches shine, –
    Why, by the verities on thee made good,
    May they not be my oracles as well,
    And set me up in hope? But hush; no more.

[*Sennet sounded. Enter* Macbeth *as* King, Lady Macbeth
    as Queen; Lennox, Ross, Lords, Ladies, *and* Attendants.]

Macbeth. Here's our chief guest.
Lady Macbeth. If he had been forgotten,
    It had been as a gap in our great feast,
    And all-thing unbecoming.
Macbeth. To-night we hold a solemn supper, sir,
    And I'll request your presence.
Banquo. Let your highness
    Command upon me; to the which my duties
    Are with a most indissoluble tie
    For ever knit.

Macbeth. Ride you this afternoon?
Banquo. Ay, my good lord.
Macbeth. We should have else desir'd your good advice, –
    Which still hath been both grave and prosperous, –
    In this day's council; but we'll take to-morrow.
    Is't far you ride?
Banquo. As far, my lord, as will fill up the time
    'Twixt this and supper: go not my horse the better,
    I must become a borrower of the night,
    For a dark hour or twain.
Macbeth. Fail not our feast.
Banquo. My lord, I will not.
Macbeth. We hear our bloody cousins are bestow'd
    In England and in Ireland; not confessing
    Their cruel parricide, filling their hearers
    With strange invention: but of that to-morrow;
    When therewithal we shall have cause of state
    Craving us jointly. Hie you to horse: adieu,
    Till you return at night. Goes Fleance with you?
Banquo. Ay, my good lord: our time does call upon's.
Macbeth. I wish your horses swift and sure of foot;
    And so I do commend you to their backs.
    Farewell. –

[*Exit* Banquo.]

    Let every man be master of his time
    Till seven at night; to make society
    The sweeter welcome, we will keep ourself
    Till supper time alone: while then, God be with you!

[*Exeunt* Lady Macbeth, Lords, Ladies, &c.]

    Sirrah, a word with you: attend those men
    Our pleasure?
Attendant. They are, my lord, without the palace gate.
Macbeth. Bring them before us.

[*Exit* Attendant.]

To be thus is nothing;
But to be safely thus: – our fears in *Banquo*.
Stick deep; and in his royalty of nature
Reigns that which would be fear'd: 'tis much he dares;
And, to that dauntless temper of his mind,
He hath a wisdom that doth guide his valour
To act in safety. There is none but he
Whose being I do fear: and under him,
My genius is rebuk'd; as, it is said,
Mark Antony's was by Caesar. He chid the sisters
When first they put the name of king upon me,
And bade them speak to him; then, prophet-like,
They hail'd him father to a line of kings:
Upon my head they plac'd a fruitless crown,
And put a barren sceptre in my gripe,
Thence to be wrench'd with an unlineal hand,
No son of mine succeeding. If 't be so,
For Banquo's issue have I fil'd my mind;
For them the gracious Duncan have I murder'd;
Put rancours in the vessel of my peace
Only for them; and mine eternal jewel
Given to the common enemy of man,
To make them kings, the seed of Banquo kings!
Rather than so, come, fate, into the list,
And champion me to the utterance! – Who's there? –

[*Re-enter* Attendant,
with two Murderers.]

Now go to the door, and stay there till we call.

[*Exit* Attendant.]

Was it not yesterday we spoke together?
First Murderer. It was, so please your highness.
Macbeth. Well then, now
Have you consider'd of my speeches? Know
That it was he, in the times past, which held you
So under fortune; which you thought had been
Our innocent self: this I made good to you
In our last conference, pass'd in probation with you

How you were borne in hand, how cross'd, the instruments,
　　Who wrought with them, and all things else that might
　　To half a soul and to a notion craz'd
　　Say, "Thus did Banquo."
First Murderer. You made it known to us.
Macbeth. I did so; and went further, which is now
　　Our point of second meeting. Do you find
　　Your patience so predominant in your nature,
　　That you can let this go? Are you so gospell'd,
　　To pray for this good man and for his issue,
　　Whose heavy hand hath bow'd you to the grave,
　　And beggar'd yours forever?
First Murderer. We are men, my liege.
Macbeth. Ay, in the catalogue ye go for men;
　　As hounds, and greyhounds, mongrels, spaniels, curs,
　　Shoughs, water-rugs, and demi-wolves are clept
　　All by the name of dogs: the valu'd file
　　Distinguishes the swift, the slow, the subtle,
　　The house-keeper, the hunter, every one
　　According to the gift which bounteous nature
　　Hath in him clos'd; whereby he does receive
　　Particular addition, from the bill
　　That writes them all alike: and so of men.
　　Now, if you have a station in the file,
　　Not i' the worst rank of manhood, say it;
　　And I will put that business in your bosoms,
　　Whose execution takes your enemy off;
　　Grapples you to the heart and love of us,
　　Who wear our health but sickly in his life,
　　Which in his death were perfect.
Second Murderer. I am one, my liege,
　　Whom the vile blows and buffets of the world
　　Have so incens'd that I am reckless what
　　I do to spite the world.
First Murderer. And I another,
　　So weary with disasters, tugg'd with fortune,
　　That I would set my life on any chance,
　　To mend it or be rid on't.
Macbeth. Both of you
　　Know Banquo was your enemy.
Both Murderers. True, my lord.

Macbeth. So is he mine; and in such bloody distance,
    That every minute of his being thrusts
    Against my near'st of life; and though I could
    With barefac'd power sweep him from my sight,
    And bid my will avouch it, yet I must not,
    For certain friends that are both his and mine,
    Whose loves I may not drop, but wail his fall
    Who I myself struck down: and thence it is
    That I to your assistance do make love;
    Masking the business from the common eye
    For sundry weighty reasons.
Second Murderer. We shall, my lord,
    Perform what you command us.
First Murderer. Though our lives –
Macbeth. Your spirits shine through you. Within this hour at most,
    I will advise you where to plant yourselves;
    Acquaint you with the perfect spy o' the time,
    The moment on't; for't must be done to-night
    And something from the palace; always thought
    That I require a clearness; and with him, –
    To leave no rubs nor botches in the work, –
    Fleance his son, that keeps him company,
    Whose absence is no less material to me
    Than is his father's, must embrace the fate
    Of that dark hour. Resolve yourselves apart:
    I'll come to you anon.
Both Murderers. We are resolv'd, my lord.
Macbeth. I'll call upon you straight: abide within.

[*Exeunt* Murderers.]

It is concluded: – Banquo, thy soul's flight,
If it find heaven, must find it out to-night.

[*Exit.*]

SCENE TWO

The same. Another Room in the Palace.

[*Enter* Lady Macbeth *and a* Servant.]

Lady Macbeth. Is Banquo gone from court?
Servant. Ay, madam, but returns again to-night.
Lady Macbeth. Say to the king, I would attend his leisure
    For a few words.
Servant. Madam, I will.

[*Exit.*]

Lady Macbeth. Naught's had, all's spent,
    Where our desire is got without content:
    'Tis safer to be that which we destroy,
    Than, by destruction, dwell in doubtful joy.

[*Enter* Macbeth.]

    How now, my lord! why do you keep alone,
    Of sorriest fancies your companions making;
    Using those thoughts which should indeed have died
    With them they think on? Things without all remedy
    Should be without regard: what's done is done.
Macbeth. We have scotch'd the snake, not kill'd it;
    She'll close, and be herself; whilst our poor malice
    Remains in danger of her former tooth.
    But let the frame of things disjoint,

Both the worlds suffer,
Ere we will eat our meal in fear, and sleep
In the affliction of these terrible dreams
That shake us nightly: better be with the dead,
Whom we, to gain our peace, have sent to peace,
Than on the torture of the mind to lie
In restless ecstasy. Duncan is in his grave;
After life's fitful fever he sleeps well;
Treason has done his worst: nor steel, nor poison,
Malice domestic, foreign levy, nothing,
Can touch him further.

Lady Macbeth. Come on;
Gently my lord, sleek o'er your rugged looks;
Be bright and jovial 'mong your guests to-night.

Macbeth. So shall I, love; and so, I pray, be you:
Let your remembrance apply to Banquo;
Present him eminence, both with eye and tongue:
Unsafe the while, that we
Must lave our honors in these flattering streams;
And make our faces vizards to our hearts,
Disguising what they are.

Lady Macbeth. You must leave this.

Macbeth. O, full of scorpions is my mind, dear wife!
Thou know'st that Banquo, and his Fleance, lives.

Lady Macbeth. But in them nature's copy's not eterne.

Macbeth. There's comfort yet; they are assailable;
Then be thou jocund: ere the bat hath flown
His cloister'd flight, ere to black Hecate's summons,
The shard-borne beetle, with his drowsy hums,
Hath rung night's yawning peal, there shall be done
A deed of dreadful note.

Lady Macbeth. What's to be done?

Macbeth. Be innocent of the knowledge, dearest chuck,
Till thou applaud the deed. Come, seeling night,
Scarf up the tender eye of pitiful day;
And with thy bloody and invisible hand
Cancel and tear to pieces that great bond
Which keeps me pale! – Light thickens; and the crow
Makes wing to the rooky wood:
Good things of day begin to droop and drowse;
Whiles night's black agents to their preys do rouse. –

Thou marvell'st at my words: but hold thee still;
Things bad begun make strong themselves by ill:
So, pr'ythee, go with me.

[*Exeunt.*]

SCENE THREE

The same. A Park or Lawn, with a gate leading to the Palace.

[*Enter three* Murderers.]

First Murderer. But who did bid thee join with us?
Third Murderer. Macbeth.
Second Murderer. He needs not our mistrust; since he delivers
    Our offices and what we have to do
    To the direction just.
First Murderer. Then stand with us.
    The west yet glimmers with some streaks of day:
    Now spurs the lated traveller apace,
    To gain the timely inn; and near approaches
    The subject of our watch.
Third Murderer. Hark! I hear horses.
Banquo. [*Within.*]
    Give us a light there, ho!
Second Murderer. Then 'tis he; the rest
    That are within the note of expectation
    Already are i' the court.
First Murderer. His horses go about.
Third Murderer. Almost a mile; but he does usually,
    So all men do, from hence to the palace gate
    Make it their walk.
Second Murderer. A light, a light!
Third Murderer. 'Tis he.
First Murderer. Stand to't.

[*Enter* Banquo, *and* Fleance *with a torch.*]

Banquo. It will be rain to-night.
First Murderer. Let it come down.

[*Assaults* Banquo.]

Banquo. O, treachery! Fly, good Fleance, fly, fly, fly!
  Thou mayst revenge. – O slave!

[*Dies.* Fleance *escapes.*]

Third Murderer. Who did strike out the light?
First Murderer. Was't not the way?
Third Murderer. There's but one down: the son is fled.
Second Murderer. We have lost best half of our affair.
First Murderer. Well, let's away, and say how much is done.

[*Exeunt.*]

SCENE FOUR

The same. A Room of state in the Palace. A banquet prepared.

[*Enter* Macbeth, Lady Macbeth, Ross, Lennox, Lords, *and* Attendants.]

Macbeth. You know your own degrees: sit down. At first
    And last the hearty welcome.
Lords. Thanks to your majesty.
Macbeth. Ourself will mingle with society,
    And play the humble host.
    Our hostess keeps her state; but, in best time,
    We will require her welcome.
Lady Macbeth. Pronounce it for me, sir, to all our friends;
    For my heart speaks they are welcome.
Macbeth. See, they encounter thee with their hearts' thanks. –
    Both sides are even: here I'll sit i' the midst:

[*Enter first* Murderer *to the door.*]

    Be large in mirth; anon we'll drink a measure
    The table round. – There's blood upon thy face.
Murderer. 'Tis Banquo's then.
Macbeth. 'Tis better thee without than he within.
    Is he despatch'd?
Murderer. My lord, his throat is cut; that I did for him.
Macbeth. Thou art the best o' the cut-throats; yet he's good
    That did the like for Fleance: if thou didst it,
    Thou art the nonpareil.
Murderer. Most royal sir,
    Fleance is 'scap'd.

Macbeth. Then comes my fit again: I had else been perfect;
  Whole as the marble, founded as the rock;
  As broad and general as the casing air:
  But now I am cabin'd, cribb'd, confin'd, bound in
  To saucy doubts and fears. But Banquo's safe?
Murderer. Ay, my good lord: safe in a ditch he bides,
  With twenty trenched gashes on his head;
  The least a death to nature.
Macbeth. Thanks for that:
  There the grown serpent lies; the worm that's fled
  Hath nature that in time will venom breed,
  No teeth for the present. – Get thee gone; to-morrow
  We'll hear, ourselves, again.

[*Exit* Murderer.]

Lady Macbeth. My royal lord,
  You do not give the cheer: the feast is sold
  That is not often vouch'd, while 'tis a-making,
  'Tis given with welcome; to feed were best at home;
  From thence the sauce to meat is ceremony;
  Meeting were bare without it.
Macbeth. Sweet remembrancer! –
  Now, good digestion wait on appetite,
  And health on both!
Lennox. May't please your highness sit.

[*The* Ghost *of* Banquo *rises, and sits in* Macbeth's *place.*]

Macbeth. Here had we now our country's honor roof'd,
  Were the grac'd person of our Banquo present;
  Who may I rather challenge for unkindness
  Than pity for mischance!
Ross. His absence, sir,
  Lays blame upon his promise. Please't your highness
  To grace us with your royal company?
Macbeth. The table's full.
Lennox. Here is a place reserv'd, sir.
Macbeth. Where?
Lennox. Here, my good lord. What is't that moves your highness?
Macbeth. Which of you have done this?

Lords. What, my good lord?

Macbeth. Thou canst not say I did it: never shake
Thy gory locks at me.

Ross. Gentlemen, rise; his highness is not well.

Lady Macbeth. Sit, worthy friends: – my lord is often thus,
And hath been from his youth: pray you, keep seat;
The fit is momentary; upon a thought
He will again be well: if much you note him,
You shall offend him, and extend his passion:
Feed, and regard him not. – Are you a man?

Macbeth. Ay, and a bold one, that dare look on that
Which might appal the devil.

Lady Macbeth. O proper stuff!
This is the very painting of your fear:
This is the air-drawn dagger which, you said,
Led you to Duncan. O, these flaws, and starts, –
Impostors to true fear, – would well become
A woman's story at a winter's fire,
Authoriz'd by her grandam. Shame itself!
Why do you make such faces? When all's done,
You look but on a stool.

Macbeth. Pr'ythee, see there! behold! look! lo! how say you? –
Why, what care I? If thou canst nod, speak too. –
If charnel houses and our graves must send
Those that we bury back, our monuments
Shall be the maws of kites.

[Ghost *disappears.*]

Lady Macbeth. What, quite unmann'd in folly?

Macbeth. If I stand here, I saw him.

Lady Macbeth. Fie, for shame!

Macbeth. Blood hath been shed ere now, i' the olden time,
Ere humane statute purg'd the gentle weal;
Ay, and since too, murders have been perform'd
Too terrible for the ear: the time has been,
That, when the brains were out, the man would die,
And there an end; but now they rise again,
With twenty mortal murders on their crowns,
And push us from our stools: this is more strange
Than such a murder is.

Lady Macbeth. My worthy lord,
  Your noble friends do lack you.
Macbeth. I do forget: –
  Do not muse at me, my most worthy friends;
  I have a strange infirmity, which is nothing
  To those that know me. Come, love and health to all;
  Then I'll sit down. – Give me some wine, fill full. –
  I drink to the general joy o' the whole table,
  And to our dear friend Banquo, whom we miss:
  Would he were here! to all, and him, we thirst,
  And all to all.
Lords. Our duties, and the pledge.

[Ghost *rises again.*]

Macbeth. Avaunt! and quit my sight! let the earth hide thee!
  Thy bones are marrowless, thy blood is cold;
  Thou hast no speculation in those eyes
  Which thou dost glare with!
Lady Macbeth. Think of this, good peers,
  But as a thing of custom: 'tis no other,
  Only it spoils the pleasure of the time.
Macbeth. What man dare, I dare:
  Approach thou like the rugged Russian bear,
  The arm'd rhinoceros, or the Hyrcan tiger;
  Take any shape but that, and my firm nerves
  Shall never tremble: or be alive again,
  And dare me to the desert with thy sword;
  If trembling I inhabit then, protest me
  The baby of a girl. Hence, horrible shadow!
  Unreal mockery, hence!

[Ghost *disappears.*]

  Why, so; – being gone,
  I am a man again. – Pray you, sit still.
Lady Macbeth. You have displaced the mirth, broke the good meeting,
  With most admir'd disorder.
Macbeth. Can such things be,
  And overcome us like a summer's cloud,
  Without our special wonder? You make me strange

Even to the disposition that I owe,
When now I think you can behold such sights,
And keep the natural ruby of your cheeks,
When mine are blanch'd with fear.
Ross. What sights, my lord?
Lady Macbeth. I pray you, speak not; he grows worse and worse;
    Question enrages him: at once, good-night: –
    Stand not upon the order of your going,
    But go at once.
Lennox. Good-night; and better health
    Attend his majesty!
Lady Macbeth. A kind good-night to all!

[*Exeunt all* Lords *and* Atendants.]

Macbeth. It will have blood; they say, blood will have blood:
    Stones have been known to move, and trees to speak;
    Augurs, and understood relations, have
    By magot-pies, and choughs, and rooks, brought forth
    The secret'st man of blood. – What is the night?
Lady Macbeth. Almost at odds with morning, which is which.
Macbeth. How say'st thou, that Macduff denies his person
    At our great bidding?
Lady Macbeth. Did you send to him, sir?
Macbeth. I hear it by the way; but I will send:
    There's not a one of them but in his house
    I keep a servant fee'd. I will to-morrow,
    (And betimes I will) to the weird sisters:
    More shall they speak; for now I am bent to know,
    By the worst means, the worst. For mine own good,
    All causes shall give way: I am in blood
    Step't in so far that, should I wade no more,
    Returning were as tedious as go o'er:
    Strange things I have in head, that will to hand;
    Which must be acted ere they may be scann'd.
Lady Macbeth. You lack the season of all natures, sleep.
Macbeth. Come, we'll to sleep. My strange and self-abuse
    Is the initiate fear that wants hard use: –
    We are yet but young in deed.

[*Exeunt.*]

SCENE FIVE

The heath.

[*Thunder. Enter the three* Witches, *meeting* Hecate.]

First Witch. Why, how now, Hecate? you look angerly.
Hecate. Have I not reason, beldams as you are,
    Saucy and overbold? How did you dare
    To trade and traffic with Macbeth
    In riddles and affairs of death;
    And I, the mistress of your charms,
    The close contriver of all harms,
    Was never call'd to bear my part,
    Or show the glory of our art?
    And, which is worse, all you have done
    Hath been but for a wayward son,
    Spiteful and wrathful; who, as others do,
    Loves for his own ends, not for you.
    But make amends now: get you gone,
    And at the pit of Acheron
    Meet me i' the morning: thither he
    Will come to know his destiny.
    Your vessels and your spells provide,
    Your charms, and everything beside.
    I am for the air; this night I'll spend
    Unto a dismal and a fatal end.
    Great business must be wrought ere noon:
    Upon the corner of the moon
    There hangs a vaporous drop profound;
    I'll catch it ere it come to ground:

And that, distill'd by magic sleights,
Shall raise such artificial sprites,
As, by the strength of their illusion,
Shall draw him on to his confusion:
He shall spurn fate, scorn death, and bear
His hopes 'bove wisdom, grace, and fear:
And you all know, security
Is mortals' chiefest enemy.

[*Music and song within, "Come away, come away" &c.*]

Hark! I am call'd; my little spirit, see,
Sits in a foggy cloud and stays for me.

[*Exit.*]

First Witch. Come, let's make haste; she'll soon be back again.

[*Exeunt.*]

SCENE SIX

Forres. A Room in the Palace.

[*Enter* Lennox *and another* Lord.]

Lennox. My former speeches have but hit your thoughts,
    Which can interpret further: only, I say,
    Thing's have been strangely borne. The gracious Duncan
    Was pitied of Macbeth: – marry, he was dead: –
    And the right valiant Banquo walk'd too late;
    Whom, you may say, if't please you, Fleance kill'd,
    For Fleance fled. Men must not walk too late.
    Who cannot want the thought, how monstrous
    It was for Malcolm and for Donalbain
    To kill their gracious father? damned fact!
    How it did grieve Macbeth! did he not straight,
    In pious rage, the two delinquents tear
    That were the slaves of drink and thralls of sleep?
    Was not that nobly done? Ay, and wisely too;
    For 'twould have anger'd any heart alive,
    To hear the men deny't. So that, I say,
    He has borne all things well: and I do think,
    That had he Duncan's sons under his key, –
    As, an't please heaven, he shall not, – they should find
    What 'twere to kill a father; so should *Fleance.* But, peace! – for
    from broad words, and 'cause he fail'd
    His presence at the tyrant's feast, I hear,
    Macduff lives in disgrace. Sir, can you tell
    Where he bestows himself?

Lord. The son of Duncan,
From whom this tyrant holds the due of birth,
Lives in the English court and is receiv'd
Of the most pious Edward with such grace
That the malevolence of fortune nothing
Takes from his high respect: thither Macduff
Is gone to pray the holy king, upon his aid
To wake Northumberland, and warlike Siward:
That, by the help of these, – with Him above
To ratify the work, – we may again
Give to our tables meat, sleep to our nights;
Free from our feasts and banquets bloody knives;
Do faithful homage, and receive free honours, –
All which we pine for now: and this report
Hath so exasperate the king that he
Prepares for some attempt of war.
Lennox. Sent he to Macduff?
Lord. He did: and with an absolute "Sir, not I,"
The cloudy messenger turns me his back,
And hums, as who should say, "You'll rue the time
That clogs me with this answer."
Lennox. And that well might
Advise him to a caution, to hold what distance
His wisdom can provide. Some holy angel
Fly to the court of England, and unfold
His message ere he come; that a swift blessing
May soon return to this our suffering country
Under a hand accurs'd!
Lord. I'll send my prayers with him.

[*Exeunt.*]

Act IV.

A dark Cave. In the middle, a Caldron Boiling.

[*Thunder. Enter the three* Witches.]

First Witch. Thrice the brinded cat hath mew'd.
Second Witch. Thrice; and once the hedge-pig whin'd.
Third Witch. Harpier cries: – "tis time, 'tis time.
First Witch. Round about the caldron go;
    In the poison'd entrails throw. –
    Toad, that under cold stone,
    Days and nights has thirty-one
    Swelter'd venom sleeping got,
    Boil thou first i' the charmed pot!
All. Double, double, toil and trouble;
    Fire, burn; and caldron, bubble.
Second Witch. Fillet of a fenny snake,
    In the caldron boil and bake;
    Eye of newt, and toe of frog,
    Wool of bat, and tongue of dog,
    Adder's fork, and blind-worm's sting,
    Lizard's leg, and howlet's wing, –
    For a charm of powerful trouble,
    Like a hell-broth boil and bubble.
All. Double, double, toil and trouble;
    Fire, burn; and caldron, bubble.
Third Witch. Scale of dragon, tooth of wolf,
    Witch's mummy, maw and gulf

Of the ravin'd salt-sea shark,
Root of hemlock digg'd i' the dark,
Liver of blaspheming Jew,
Gall of goat, and slips of yew
Sliver'd in the moon's eclipse,
Nose of Turk, and Tartar's lips,
Finger of birth-strangl'd babe
Ditch-deliver'd by a drab, –
Make the gruel thick and slab:
Add thereto a tiger's chaudron,
For the ingredients of our caldron.
All. Double, double, toil and trouble;
Fire, burn; and caldron, bubble.
Second Witch. Cool it with a baboon's blood,
Then the charm is firm and good.

[*Enter* Hecate.]

Hecate. O, well done! I commend your pains;
And everyone shall share i' the gains.
And now about the cauldron sing,
Like elves and fairies in a ring,
Enchanting all that you put in.
[*Song.*
Black spirits and white, red spirits and gray;
Mingle, mingle, mingle, you that mingle may.

[*Exit* Hecate.]

Second Witch. By the pricking of my thumbs,
Something wicked this way comes: –
Open, locks, whoever knocks!

[*Enter Macbeth.*]

Macbeth. How now, you secret, black, and midnight hags!
What is't you do?
All. A deed without a name.
Macbeth. I conjure you, by that which you profess, –
Howe'er you come to know it, – answer me:
Though you untie the winds, and let them fight

Against the churches; though the yesty waves
Confound and swallow navigation up;
Though bladed corn be lodg'd, and trees blown down;
Though castles topple on their warders' heads;
Though palaces and pyramids do slope
Their heads to their foundations; though the treasure
Of nature's germins tumble all together,
Even till destruction sicken, – answer me
To what I ask you.
First Witch. Speak.
Second Witch. Demand.
Third Witch. We'll answer.
First Witch. Say, if thou'dst rather hear it from our mouths,
Or from our masters?
Macbeth. Call 'em, let me see 'em.
First Witch. Pour in sow's blood, that hath eaten
Her nine farrow; grease that's sweaten
From the murderer's gibbet throw
Into the flame.
All. Come, high or low;
Thyself and office deftly show!

[*Thunder. An* Apparition *of an armed* Head *rises.*]

Macbeth. Tell me, thou unknown power, –
First Witch. He knows thy thought:
Hear his speech, but say thou naught.
Apparition. Macbeth! Macbeth! Macbeth! Beware Macduff;
Beware the Thane of Fife. – Dismiss me: – enough.

[*Descends.*]

Macbeth. Whate'er thou art, for thy good caution, thanks;
Thou hast harp'd my fear aright: – but one word more, –
First Witch. He will not be commanded: here's another,
More potent than the first.

[*Thunder. An* Apparition *of a bloody* Child *rises.*]

Apparition. – Macbeth! Macbeth! Macbeth!
Macbeth. Had I three ears, I'd hear thee.

Apparition. Be bloody, bold, and resolute; laugh to scorn
    The power of man, for none of woman born
    Shall harm *Macbeth.*

[Descends.]

Macbeth. Then live, Macduff: what need I fear of thee?
    But yet I'll make assurance double sure,
    And take a bond of fate: thou shalt not live;
    That I may tell pale-hearted fear it lies,
    And sleep in spite of thunder. – What is this,

[Thunder. An Apparition *of a* Child *crowned,*
with a tree in his hand, rises.]

    That rises like the issue of a king,
    And wears upon his baby brow the round
    And top of sovereignty?
All. Listen, but speak not to't.
Apparition. Be lion-mettled, proud; and take no care
    Who chafes, who frets, or where conspirers are:
    Macbeth shall never vanquish'd be, until
    Great Birnam wood to high Dunsinane hill
    Shall come against him.

[Descends.]

Macbeth. That will never be:
    Who can impress the forest; bid the tree
    Unfix his earth-bound root? Sweet bodements, good!
    Rebellion's head, rise never till the wood
    Of Birnam rise, and our high-plac'd Macbeth
    Shall live the lease of nature, pay his breath
    To time and mortal custom. – Yet my heart
    Throbs to know one thing: tell me, – if your art
    Can tell so much, – shall Banquo's issue ever
    Reign in this kingdom?
All. Seek to know no more.
Macbeth. I will be satisfied: deny me this,
    And an eternal curse fall on you! Let me know: –
    Why sinks that cauldron? and what noise is this?

[*Hautboys.*]

First Witch. Show!
Second Witch. Show!
Third Witch. Show!
All. Show his eyes, and grieve his heart;
Come like shadows, so depart!

[*Eight* kings *appear, and pass over in order,
the last with a glass in his hand;*
Banquo *following.*]

Macbeth. Thou are too like the spirit of Banquo; down!
Thy crown does sear mine eyeballs: – and thy hair,
Thou other gold-bound brow, is like the first; –
A third is like the former. – Filthy hags!
Why do you show me this? – A fourth! – Start, eyes!
What, will the line stretch out to the crack of doom?
Another yet! – A seventh! – I'll see no more: –
And yet the eighth appears, who bears a glass
Which shows me many more; and some I see
That twofold balls and treble sceptres carry:
Horrible sight! – Now I see 'tis true;
For the blood-bolter'd Banquo smiles upon me,
And points at them for his. – What! is this so?
First Witch. Ay, sir, all this is so: – but why
Stands Macbeth thus amazedly? –
Come, sisters, cheer we up his sprites,
And show the best of our delights;
I'll charm the air to give a sound,
While you perform your antic round;
That this great king may kindly say,
Our duties did his welcome pay.

[*Music.* The Witches *dance, and then vanish.*]

Macbeth. Where are they? Gone? – Let this pernicious hour
Stand aye accursed in the calendar! –
Come in, without there!

[*Enter* Lennox.]

Lennox. What's your grace's will?
Macbeth. Saw you the weird sisters?
Lennox. No, my lord.
Macbeth. Came they not by you?
Lennox. No indeed, my lord.
Macbeth. Infected be the air whereon they ride;
    And damn'd all those that trust them! – I did hear
    The galloping of horse: who was't came by?
Lennox. 'Tis two or three, my lord, that bring you word
    Macduff is fled to England.
Macbeth. Fled to England!
Lennox. Ay, my good lord.
Macbeth. Time, thou anticipat'st my dread exploits:
    The flighty purpose never is o'ertook
    Unless the deed go with it: from this moment
    The very firstlings of my heart shall be
    The firstlings of my hand. And even now,
    To crown my thoughts with acts, be it thought and done:
    The castle of Macduff I will surprise;
    Seize upon Fife; give to the edge o' the sword
    His wife, his babes, and all unfortunate souls
    That trace him in his line. No boasting like a fool;
    This deed I'll do before this purpose cool:
    But no more sights! – Where are these gentlemen?
    Come, bring me where they are.

[*Exeunt.*]

Fife. A Room in Macduff's *Castle.*

[*Enter* Lady Macduff, *her* Son, *and* Ross.]

Lady Macduff. What had he done, to make him fly the land?
Ross. You must have patience, madam.
Lady Macduff. He had none:
    His flight was madness: when our actions do not,
    Our fears do make us traitors.
Ross. You know not
    Whether it was his wisdom or his fear.
Lady Macduff. Wisdom! to leave his wife, to leave his babes,
    His mansion, and his titles, in a place
    From whence himself does fly? He loves us not:
    He wants the natural touch; for the poor wren,
    The most diminutive of birds, will fight,
    Her young ones in her nest, against the owl.
    All is the fear, and nothing is the love;
    As little is the wisdom, where the flight
    So runs against all reason.
Ross. My dearest coz,
    I pray you, school yourself: but, for your husband,
    He is noble, wise, Judicious, and best knows
    The fits o' the season. I dare not speak much further:
    But cruel are the times, when we are traitors,
    And do not know ourselves; when we hold rumour
    From what we fear, yet know not what we fear,
    But float upon a wild and violent sea
    Each way and move. – I take my leave of you:
    Shall not be long but I'll be here again:
    Things at the worst will cease, or else climb upward

To what they were before. – My pretty cousin,
    Blessing upon you!
Lady Macduff. Father'd he is, and yet he's fatherless.
Ross. I am so much a fool, should I stay longer,
    It would be my disgrace and your discomfort:
    I take my leave at once.

[*Exit.*]

Lady Macduff. Sirrah, your father's dead;
    And what will you do now? How will you live?
Son. As birds do, mother.
Lady Macduff. What, with worms and flies?
Son. With what I get, I mean; and so do they.
Lady Macduff. Poor bird! thou'dst never fear the net nor lime,
    The pit-fall nor the gin.
Son. Why should I, mother? Poor birds they are not set for.
    My father is not dead, for all your saying.
Lady Macduff. Yes, he is dead: how wilt thou do for father?
Son. Nay, how will you do for a husband?
Lady Macduff. Why, I can buy me twenty at any market.
Son. Then you'll buy 'em to sell again.
Lady Macduff. Thou speak'st with all thy wit; and yet, i' faith,
    With wit enough for thee.
Son. Was my father a traitor, mother?
Lady Macduff. Ay, that he was.
Son. What is a traitor?
Lady Macduff. Why, one that swears and lies.
Son. And be all traitors that do so?
Lady Macduff. Everyone that does so is a traitor, and must be
    hanged.
Son. And must they all be hanged that swear and lie?
Lady Macduff. Every one.
Son. Who must hang them?
Lady Macduff. Why, the honest men.
Son. Then the liars and swearers are fools: for there are liars and
    swearers enow to beat the honest men and hang up them.
Lady Macduff. Now, God help thee, poor monkey! But how wilt
    thou do for a father?
Son. If he were dead, you'ld weep for him: if you would not, it were a
    good sign that I should quickly have a new father.

Lady Macduff. Poor prattler, how thou talk'st!

[*Enter a* Messenger.]

Messenger. Bless you, fair dame! I am not to you known,
    Though in your state of honor I am perfect.
    I doubt some danger does approach you nearly:
    If you will take a homely man's advice,
    Be not found here; hence, with your little ones.
    To fright you thus, methinks, I am too savage;
    To do worse to you were fell cruelty,
    Which is too nigh your person. Heaven preserve you!
    I dare abide no longer.

[*Exit.*]

Lady Macduff. Whither should I fly?
    I have done no harm. But I remember now
    I am in this earthly world; where to do harm
    Is often laudable; to do good sometime
    Accounted dangerous folly: why then, alas,
    Do I put up that womanly defence,
    To say I have done no harm? – What are these faces?

[*Enter* Murderers.]

First Murderer. Where is your husband?
Lady Macduff. I hope, in no place so unsanctified
    Where such as thou mayst find him.
First Murderer. He's a traitor.
Son. Thou liest, thou shag-haar'd villain!
First Murderer. What, you egg!

[*Stabbing him.*]

    Young fry of treachery!
Son. He has kill'd me, mother:
    Run away, I pray you!

[*Dies.* Exit Lady Macduff, crying Murder,
        and pursued by the Murderers.]

SCENE THREE

England. Before the King's *Palace.*

[*Enter* Malcolm *and* Macduff.]

Malcolm. Let us seek out some desolate shade and there
    Weep our sad bosoms empty.
Macduff. Let us rather
    Hold fast the mortal sword, and, like good men,
    Bestride our down-fall'n birthdom: each new morn
    New widows howl; new orphans cry; new sorrows
    Strike heaven on the face, that it resounds
    As if it felt with Scotland, and yell'd out
    Like syllable of dolour.
Malcolm. What I believe, I'll wail;
    What know, believe; and what I can redress,
    As I shall find the time to friend, I will.
    What you have spoke, it may be so perchance.
    This tyrant, whose sole name blisters our tongues,
    Was once thought honest: you have loved him well;
    He hath not touch'd you yet. I am young; but something
    You may deserve of him through me; and wisdom
    To offer up a weak, poor, innocent lamb
    To appease an angry god.
Macduff. I am not treacherous.
Malcolm. But Macbeth is.
    A good and virtuous nature may recoil
    In an imperial charge. But I shall crave your pardon;
    That which you are, my thoughts cannot transpose;

Angels are bright still, though the brightest fell:
Though all things foul would wear the brows of grace,
Yet grace must still look so.
Macduff. I have lost my hopes.
Malcolm. Perchance even there where I did find my doubts.
Why in that rawness left you wife and child, –
Those precious motives, those strong knots of love, –
Without leave-taking? – I pray you,
Let not my jealousies be your dishonors,
But mine own safeties: – you may be rightly just,
Whatever I shall think.
Macduff. Bleed, bleed, poor country!
Great tyranny, lay thou thy basis sure,
For goodness dare not check thee! wear thou thy wrongs,
The title is affeer'd. – Fare thee well, lord:
I would not be the villain that thou think'st
For the whole space that's in the tyrant's grasp
And the rich East to boot.
Malcolm. Be not offended:
I speak not as in absolute fear of you.
I think our country sinks beneath the yoke;
It weeps, it bleeds; and each new day a gash
Is added to her wounds. I think, withal,
There would be hands uplifted in my right;
And here, from gracious England, have I offer
Of goodly thousands: but, for all this,
When I shall tread upon the tyrant's head,
Or wear it on my sword, yet my poor country
Shall have more vices than it had before;
More suffer, and more sundry ways than ever,
By him that shall succeed.
Macduff. What should he be?
Malcolm. It is myself I mean: in whom I know
All the particulars of vice so grafted
That, when they shall be open'd, black Macbeth
Will seem as pure as snow; and the poor state
Esteem him as a lamb, being compar'd
With my confineless harms.
Macduff. Not in the legions
Of horrid hell can come a devil more damn'd
In evils to top *Macbeth.*

Malcolm. I grant him bloody,
 Luxurious, avaricious, false, deceitful,
 Sudden, malicious, smacking of every sin
 That has a name: but there's no bottom, none,
 In my voluptuousness: your wives, your daughters,
 Your matrons, and your maids, could not fill up
 The cistern of my lust; and my desire
 All continent impediments would o'erbear,
 That did oppose my will: better Macbeth
 Than such an one to reign.

Macduff. Boundless intemperance
 In nature is a tyranny; it hath been
 The untimely emptying of the happy throne,
 And fall of many kings. But fear not yet
 To take upon you what is yours: you may
 Convey your pleasures in a spacious plenty,
 And yet seem cold, the time you may so hoodwink.
 We have willing dames enough; there cannot be
 That vulture in you, to devour so many
 As will to greatness dedicate themselves,
 Finding it so inclin'd.

Malcolm. With this there grows,
 In my most ill-compos'd affection, such
 A stanchless avarice, that, were I king,
 I should cut off the nobles for their lands;
 Desire his jewels, and this other's house:
 And my more-having would be as a sauce
 To make me hunger more; that I should forge
 Quarrels unjust against the good and loyal,
 Destroying them for wealth.

Macduff. This avarice
 Sticks deeper; grows with more pernicious root
 Than summer-seeming lust; and it hath been
 The sword of our slain kings: yet do not fear;
 Scotland hath foysons to fill up your will,
 Of your mere own: all these are portable,
 With other graces weigh'd.

Malcolm. But I have none: the king-becoming graces,
 As justice, verity, temperance, stableness,
 Bounty, perseverance, mercy, lowliness,
 Devotion, patience, courage, fortitude,

I have no relish of them; but abound
In the division of each several crime,
Acting it many ways. Nay, had I power, I should
Pour the sweet milk of concord into hell,
Uproar the universal peace, confound
All unity on earth.
Macduff. O Scotland, Scotland!
Malcolm. If such a one be fit to govern, speak:
I am as I have spoken.
Macduff. Fit to govern!
No, not to live! – O nation miserable,
With an untitled tyrant bloody-scepter'd,
When shalt thou see thy wholesome days again,
Since that the truest issue of thy throne
By his own interdiction stands accurs'd
And does blaspheme his breed? – Thy royal father
Was a most sainted king; the queen that bore thee,
Oftener upon her knees than on her feet,
Died every day she lived. Fare-thee-well!
These evils thou repeat'st upon thyself
Have banish'd me from Scotland. – O my breast,
Thy hope ends here!
Malcolm. Macduff, this noble passion,
Child of integrity, hath from my soul
Wiped the black scruples, reconcil'd my thoughts
To thy good truth and honour. Devilish Macbeth
By many of these trains hath sought to win me
Into his power; and modest wisdom plucks me
From over-credulous haste: but God above
Deal between thee and me! for even now
I put myself to thy direction, and
Unspeak mine own detraction; here abjure
The taints and blames I laid upon myself,
For strangers to my nature. I am yet
Unknown to woman; never was forsworn;
Scarcely have coveted what was mine own;
At no time broke my faith; would not betray
The devil to his fellow; and delight
No less in truth than life: my first false speaking
Was this upon myself: – what I am truly,
Is thine and my poor country's to command:

Whither, indeed, before thy here-approach,
Old Siward, with ten thousand warlike men
Already at a point, was setting forth:
Now we'll together; and the chance of goodness
Be like our warranted quarrel! Why are you silent?
Macduff. Such welcome and unwelcome things at once
'Tis hard to reconcile.

[*Enter a* Doctor.]

Malcolm. Well; more anon. – Comes the king forth, I pray you?
Doctor. Ay, sir: there are a crew of wretched souls
    That stay his cure: their malady convinces
    The great assay of art; but, at his touch,
    Such sanctity hath heaven given his hand,
    They presently amend.
Malcolm. I thank you, doctor.

[*Exit* Doctor.]

Macduff. What's the disease he means?
Malcolm. 'Tis call'd the evil:
    A most miraculous work in this good king;
    Which often, since my here-remain in England,
    I have seen him do. How he solicits heaven,
    Himself best knows: but strangely-visited people,
    All swoln and ulcerous, pitiful to the eye,
    The mere despair of surgery, he cures;
    Hanging a golden stamp about their necks,
    Put on with holy prayers: and 'tis spoken,
    To the succeeding royalty he leaves
    The healing benediction. With this strange virtue,
    He hath a heavenly gift of prophecy;
    And sundry blessings hang about his throne,
    That speak him full of grace.
Macduff. See, who comes here?
Malcolm. My countryman; but yet I know him not.

[*Enter* Ross.]

Macduff. My ever-gentle cousin, welcome hither.

Malcolm. I know him now. Good God, betimes remove
    The means that makes us strangers!
Ross. Sir, amen.
Macduff. Stands Scotland where it did?
Ross. Alas, poor country, –
    Almost afraid to know itself! It cannot
    Be call'd our mother, but our grave: where nothing,
    But who knows nothing, is once seen to smile;
    Where sighs, and groans, and shrieks, that rent the air,
    Are made, not mark'd; where violent sorrow seems
    A modern ecstasy; the dead man's knell
    Is there scarce ask'd for who; and good men's lives
    Expire before the flowers in their caps,
    Dying or ere they sicken.
Macduff. O, relation
    Too nice, and yet too true!
Malcolm. What's the newest grief?
Ross. That of an hour's age doth hiss the speaker;
    Each minute teems a new one.
Macduff. How does my wife?
Ross. Why, well.
Macduff. And all my children?
Ross. Well too.
Macduff. The tyrant has not batter'd at their peace?
Ross. No; they were well at peace when I did leave 'em.
Macduff. Be not a niggard of your speech: how goes't?
Ross. When I came hither to transport the tidings,
    Which I have heavily borne, there ran a rumour
    Of many worthy fellows that were out;
    Which was to my belief witness'd the rather,
    For that I saw the tyrant's power a-foot:
    Now is the time of help; your eye in Scotland
    Would create soldiers, make our women fight,
    To doff their dire distresses.
Malcolm. Be't their comfort
    We are coming thither: gracious England hath
    Lent us good Siward and ten thousand men;
    An older and a better soldier none
    That Christendom gives out.
Ross. Would I could answer
    This comfort with the like! But I have words

That would be howl'd out in the desert air,
Where hearing should not latch them.
Macduff. What concern they?
    The general cause? or is it a fee-grief
    Due to some single breast?
Ross. No mind that's honest
    But in it shares some woe; though the main part
    Pertains to you alone.
Macduff. If it be mine,
    Keep it not from me, quickly let me have it.
Ross. Let not your ears despise my tongue for ever,
    Which shall possess them with the heaviest sound
    That ever yet they heard.
Macduff. Humh! I guess at it.
Ross. Your castle is surpris'd; your wife and babes
    Savagely slaughter'd: to relate the manner
    Were, on the quarry of these murder'd deer,
    To add the death of you.
Malcolm. Merciful heaven! –
    What, man! ne'er pull your hat upon your brows;
    Give sorrow words: the grief that does not speak
    Whispers the o'er-fraught heart, and bids it break.
Macduff. My children too?
Ross. Wife, children, servants, all
    That could be found.
Macduff. And I must be from thence!
    My wife kill'd too?
Ross. I have said.
Malcolm. Be comforted:
    Let's make us medicines of our great revenge,
    To cure this deadly grief.
Macduff. He has no children. – All my pretty ones?
    Did you say all? – O hell-kite! – All?
    What, all my pretty chickens and their dam
    At one fell swoop?
Malcolm. Dispute it like a man.
Macduff. I shall do so;
    But I must also feel it as a man:
    I cannot but remember such things were,
    That were most precious to me. – Did heaven look on,
    And would not take their part? Sinful Macduff,

They were all struck for thee! naught that I am,
Not for their own demerits, but for mine,
Fell slaughter on their souls: heaven rest them now!
Malcolm. Be this the whetstone of your sword. Let grief
    Convert to anger; blunt not the heart, enrage it.
Macduff. O, I could play the woman with mine eye,
    And braggart with my tongue! – But, gentle heavens,
    Cut short all intermission; front to front
    Bring thou this fiend of Scotland and myself;
    Within my sword's length set him; if he 'scape,
    Heaven forgive him too!
Malcolm. This tune goes manly.
    Come, go we to the king; our power is ready;
    Our lack is nothing but our leave: Macbeth
    Is ripe for shaking, and the powers above
    Put on their instruments. Receive what cheer you may;
    The night is long that never finds the day.

[*Exeunt.*]

Act V.

SCENE ONE

Dunsinane. A Room in the Castle.

[*Enter a* Doctor of Physic *and a* Waiting-Gentlewoman.]

Doctor. I have two nights watched with you, but can perceive no
truth in your report. When was it she last walked?

Gentlewoman. Since his majesty went into the field, I have seen her
rise from her bed, throw her nightgown upon her, unlock her closet, take forth paper, fold it, write upon it, read it, afterwards seal it,
and again return to bed; yet all this while in a most fast sleep.

Doctor. A great perturbation in nature, – to receive at once the benefit of sleep, and do the effects of watching – In this slumbery agi-
tation, besides her walking and other actual performances, what, at
any time, have you heard her say?

Gentlewoman. That, sir, which I will not report after her.

Doctor. You may to me; and 'tis most meet you should.

Gentlewoman. Neither to you nor any one; having no witness to
confirm my speech. Lo you, here she comes!

[*Enter* Lady Macbeth, *with a taper.*]

This is her very guise; and, upon my life, fast asleep. Observe her;
stand close.

Doctor. How came she by that light?

Gentlewoman. Why, it stood by her: she has light by her continually;
'tis her command.

Doctor. You see, her eyes are open.

Gentlewoman. Ay, but their sense is shut.

Doctor. What is it she does now? Look how she rubs her hands.

Gentlewoman. It is an accustomed action with her, to seem thus washing her hands: I have known her continue in this a quarter of an hour.

Lady Macbeth. Yet here's a spot.

Doctor. Hark, she speaks: I will set down what comes from her, to satisfy my remembrance the more strongly.

Lady Macbeth. Out, damned spot! out, I say! – One; two; why, then 'tis time to do't ; – Hell is murky! – Fie, my lord, fie! a soldier, and afeard? What need we fear who knows it, when none can call our power to account? – Yet who would have thought the old man to have had so much blood in him?

Doctor. Do you mark that?

Lady Macbeth. The Thane of Fife had a wife; where is she now? – What, will these hands ne'er be clean? No more o' that, my lord, no more o' that: you mar all with this starting.

Doctor. Go to, go to; you have known what you should not.

Gentlewoman. She has spoke what she should not, I am sure of that: heaven knows what she has known.

Lady Macbeth. Here's the smell of the blood still: all the perfumes of Arabia will not sweeten this little hand. Oh, oh, oh!

Doctor. What a sigh is there! The heart is sorely charged.

Gentlewoman. I would not have such a heart in my bosom for the dignity of the whole body.

Doctor. Well, well, well, –

Gentlewoman. Pray God it be, sir.

Doctor. This disease is beyond my practice: yet I have known those which have walked in their sleep who have died holily in their beds.

Lady Macbeth. Wash your hands, put on your nightgown; look not so pale: – I tell you yet again, Banquo's buried; he cannot come out on's grave.

Doctor. Even so?

Lady Macbeth. To bed, to bed; there's knocking at the gate: come, come, come, come, give me your hand: what's done cannot be undone: to bed, to bed, to bed.

[Exit.]

Doctor. Will she go now to bed?

Gentlewoman. Directly.

Doctor. Foul whisperings are abroad: unnatural deeds
    Do breed unnatural troubles: infected minds
    To their deaf pillows will discharge their secrets.
    More needs she the divine than the physician. –
    God, God, forgive us all! – Look after her;
    Remove from her the means of all annoyance,
    And still keep eyes upon her: – so, good-night:
    My mind she has mated, and amaz'd my sight:
    I think, but dare not speak.

Gentlewoman. Good-night, good doctor.

[*Exeunt.*]

SCENE TWO

The Country near Dunsinane.

[*Enter. with drum and colours,* Menteith,
Caithness, Angus, Lennox, *and* Soldiers.]

Menteith. The English power is near, led on by Malcolm,
    His uncle Siward, and the good Macduff. Revenges burn in them;
    for their dear causes
    Would to the bleeding and the grim alarm
    Excite the mortified man.
Angus. Near Birnam wood
    Shall we well meet them; that way are they coming.
Caithness. Who knows if Donalbain be with his brother?
Lennox. For certain, sir, he is not: I have a file
    Of all the gentry: there is Siward's son
    And many unrough youths, that even now
    Protest their first of manhood.
Menteith. What does the tyrant?
Caithness. Great Dunsinane he strongly fortifies:
    Some say he's mad; others, that lesser hate him,
    Do call it valiant fury: but, for certain,
    He cannot buckle his distemper'd cause
    Within the belt of rule.
Angus. Now does he feel
    His secret murders sticking on his hands;
    Now minutely revolts upbraid his faith-breach;
    Those he commands move only in command,
    Nothing in love: now does he feel his title

Hang loose about him, like a giant's robe
Upon a dwarfish thief.
Menteith. Who, then, shall blame
His pester'd senses to recoil and start,
When all that is within him does condemn
Itself for being there?
Caithness. Well, march we on,
To give obedience where 'tis truly ow'd:
Meet we the medicine of the sickly weal;
And with him pour we, in our country's purge,
Each drop of us.
Lennox. Or so much as it needs,
To dew the sovereign flower, and drown the weeds.
Make we our march towards Birnam.

[*Exeunt, marching.*]

SCENE THREE

Dunsinane. A Room in the Castle.

[*Enter* Macbeth, Doctor, *and* Attendants.]

Macbeth. Bring me no more reports; let them fly all:
  Till Birnam wood remove to Dunsinane
  I cannot taint with fear. What's the boy Malcolm?
  Was he not born of woman? The spirits that know
  All mortal consequences have pronounc'd me thus, –
  "Fear not, Macbeth; no man that's born of woman
  Shall e'er have power upon thee." – Then fly, false thanes,
  And mingle with the English epicures:
  The mind I sway by, and the heart I bear,
  Shall never sag with doubt nor shake with fear.

[*Enter a* Servant.]

  The devil damn thee black, thou cream-fac'd loon!
  Where gott'st thou that goose look?
Servant. There is ten thousand –
Macbeth. Geese, villain?
Servant. Soldiers, sir.
Macbeth. Go prick thy face and over-red thy fear,
  Thou lily-liver'd boy. What soldiers, patch?
  Death of thy soul! those linen cheeks of thine
  Are counsellors to fear. What soldiers, whey-face?
Servant. The English force, so please you.
Macbeth. Take thy face hence.

[*Exit* Servant.]

Seyton! – I am sick at heart,
 When I behold – Seyton, I say!- This push
 Will chair me ever or disseat me now.
 I have liv'd long enough: my way of life
 Is fall'n into the sear, the yellow leaf;
 And that which should accompany old age,
 As honour, love, obedience, troops of friends,
 I must not look to have; but, in their stead,
 Curses, not loud but deep, mouth-honour, breath,
 Which the poor heart would fain deny, and dare not.
 Seyton! –

[*Enter* Seyton.]

Seyton. What's your gracious pleasure?
Macbeth. What news more?
Seyton. All is confirm'd, my lord, which was reported.
Macbeth. I'll fight till from my bones my flesh be hack'd.
 Give me my armour.
Seyton. 'Tis not needed yet.
Macbeth. I'll put it on.
 Send out more horses, skirr the country round;
 Hang those that talk of fear. – Give me mine armour. –
 How does your patient, doctor?
Doctor. Not so sick, my lord,
 As she is troubled with thick-coming fancies,
 That keep her from her rest.
Macbeth. Cure her of that:
 Canst thou not minister to a mind diseas'd;
 Pluck from the memory a rooted sorrow;
 Raze out the written troubles of the brain;
 And with some sweet oblivious antidote
 Cleanse the stuff'd bosom of that perilous stuff
 Which weighs upon the heart?
Doctor. Therein the patient
 Must minister to himself.
Macbeth. Throw physic to the dogs, – I'll none of it. –
 Come, put mine armour on; give me my staff: –
 Seyton, send out. – Doctor, the Thanes fly from me. –
 Come, sir, despatch. – If thou couldst, doctor, cast
 The water of my land, find her disease,

And purge it to a sound and pristine health,
I would applaud thee to the very echo,
That should applaud again. – Pull't off, I say. –
What rhubarb, senna, or what purgative drug,
Would scour these English hence? Hear'st thou of them?
Doctor. Ay, my good lord; your royal preparation
Makes us hear something.
Macbeth. Bring it after me. –
I will not be afraid of death and bane,
Till Birnam forest come to Dunsinane.

[*Exeunt all except* Doctor.]

Doctor. Were I from Dunsinane away and clear,
Profit again should hardly draw me here.

[*Exit.*]

SCENE FOUR

Country near Dunsinane: a Wood in view.

[*Enter*, with drum and colours, Malcolm,
old Siward and his Son, Macduff, Menteith, Caithness,
Angus, Lennox, Ross, and Soldiers, marching.]

Malcolm. Cousins, I hope the days are near at hand
    That chambers will be safe.
Menteith. We doubt it nothing.
Siward. What wood is this before us?
Menteith. The wood of Birnam.
Malcolm. Let every soldier hew him down a bough,
    And bear't before him; thereby shall we shadow
    The numbers of our host, and make discovery
    Err in report of us.
Soldiers. It shall be done.
Siward. We learn no other but the confident tyrant
    Keeps still in Dunsinane, and will endure
    Our setting down before't.
Malcolm. 'Tis his main hope:
    For where there is advantage to be given,
    Both more and less have given him the revolt;
    And none serve with him but constrained things,
    Whose hearts are absent too.
Macduff. Let our just censures
    Attend the true event, and put we on
    Industrious soldiership.
Siward. The time approaches,
    That will with due decision make us know
    What we shall say we have, and what we owe.

Thoughts speculative their unsure hopes relate;
But certain issue strokes must arbitrate:
Towards which advance the war.

[*Exeunt, marching.*]

SCENE FIVE

Dunsinane. Within the castle.

[*Enter* with drum and colours, Macbeth, Seyton, and Soldiers.]

Macbeth. Hang out our banners on the outward walls;
 The cry is still, "They come:" our castle's strength
 Will laugh a siege to scorn: here let them lie
 Till famine and the ague eat them up:
 Were they not forc'd with those that should be ours,
 We might have met them dareful, beard to beard,
 And beat them backward home.

[*A cry of women within.*]

 What is that noise?
Seyton. It is the cry of women, my good lord.

[*Exit.*]

Macbeth. I have almost forgot the taste of fears:
 The time has been, my senses would have cool'd
 To hear a night-shriek; and my fell of hair
 Would at a dismal treatise rouse and stir
 As life were in't: I have supp'd full with horrors;
 Direness, familiar to my slaught'rous thoughts,
 Cannot once start me.

[*Re-enter* Seyton.]

Wherefore was that cry?
Seyton. The queen, my lord, is dead.
Macbeth. She should have died hereafter;
    There would have been a time for such a word. –
    To-morrow, and to-morrow, and to-morrow,
    Creeps in this petty pace from day to day,
    To the last syllable of recorded time;
    And all our yesterdays have lighted fools
    The way to dusty death. Out, out, brief candle!
    Life's but a walking shadow; a poor player,
    That struts and frets his hour upon the stage,
    And then is heard no more: it is a tale
    Told by an idiot, full of sound and fury,
    Signifying nothing.

[*Enter a* Messenger.]

Thou com'st to use thy tongue; thy story quickly.
Messenger. Gracious my lord,
    I should report that which I say I saw,
    But know not how to do it.
Macbeth. Well, say, sir.
Messenger. As I did stand my watch upon the hill,
    I look'd toward Birnam, and anon, methought,
    The wood began to move.
Macbeth. Liar, and slave!

[*Strikimg him.*]

Messenger. Let me endure your wrath, if't be not so.
    Within this three mile may you see it coming;
    I say, a moving grove.
Macbeth. If thou speak'st false,
    Upon the next tree shalt thou hang alive,
    Till famine cling thee: if thy speech be sooth,
    I care not if thou dost for me as much. –
    I pull in resolution; and begin
    To doubt the equivocation of the fiend
    That lies like truth. "Fear not, till Birnam wood
    Do come to Dunsinane;" and now a wood
    Comes toward Dunsinane. – Arm, arm, and out! –

If this which he avouches does appear,
There is nor flying hence nor tarrying here.
I 'gin to be a-weary of the sun,
And wish the estate o' the world were now undone. –
Ring the alarum bell! – Blow, wind! come, wrack!
At least we'll die with harness on our back.

[*Exeunt.*]

SCENE SIX

The same. A Plain before the Castle.

[*Enter*, with drum and colours, Malcolm, old Siward,
Macduff, &c., and their Army, with boughs.]

Malcolm. Now near enough; your leafy screens throw down,
  And show like those you are. – You, worthy uncle,
  Shall with my cousin, your right-noble son,
  Lead our first battle: worthy Macduff and we
  Shall take upon's what else remains to do,
  According to our order.
Siward. Fare you well. –
  Do we but find the tyrant's power to-night,
  Let us be beaten, if we cannot fight.
Macduff. Make all our trumpets speak; give them all breath,
  Those clamorous harbingers of blood and death.

[*Exeunt.*]

SCENE SEVEN

The same. Another part of the Plain.

[Alarums. Enter Macbeth.]

Macbeth. They have tied me to a stake; I cannot fly,
But, bear-like I must fight the course. – What's he
That was not born of woman? Such a one
Am I to fear, or none.

[Enter young Siward.]

Young Siward. What is thy name?
Macbeth. Thou'lt be afraid to hear it.
Young Siward. No; though thou call'st thyself a hotter name
Than any is in hell.
Macbeth. My name's *Macbeth.*
Young Siward. The devil himself could not pronounce a title
More hateful to mine ear.
Macbeth. No, nor more fearful.
Young Siward. Thou liest, abhorred tyrant; with my sword
I'll prove the lie thou speak'st.

[They fight, and young Seward is slain.]

Macbeth. Thou wast born of woman. –
But swords I smile at, weapons laugh to scorn,
Brandish'd by man that's of a woman born.

[Exit.]

[*Alarums. Enter* Macduff.]

Macduff. That way the noise is. – Tyrant, show thy face!
　If thou be'st slain and with no stroke of mine,
　My wife and children's ghosts will haunt me still.
　I cannot strike at wretched kerns, whose arms
　Are hired to bear their staves; either thou, Macbeth,
　Or else my sword, with an unbatter'd edge,
　I sheathe again undeeded. There thou shouldst be;
　By this great clatter, one of greatest note
　Seems bruited. Let me find him, fortune!
　And more I beg not.

[*Exit.* Alarums.]

[*Enter* Malcolm *and* old Siward.]

Siward. This way, my lord; – the castle's gently render'd:
　The tyrant's people on both sides do fight;
　The noble thanes do bravely in the war;
　The day almost itself professes yours,
　And little is to do.
Malcolm. We have met with foes
　That strike beside us.
Siward. Enter, sir, the castle.

[*Exeunt. Alarums.*]

SCENE EIGHT

The same. Another part of the field.

[Enter Macbeth.]

Macbeth. Why should I play the Roman fool, and die
    On mine own sword? whiles I see lives, the gashes
    Do better upon them.

[Enter Macduff.*]*

Macduff. Turn, hell-hound, turn!
Macbeth. Of all men else I have avoided thee:
    But get thee back; my soul is too much charg'd
    With blood of thine already.
Macduff. I have no words, –
    My voice is in my sword: thou bloodier villain
    Than terms can give thee out!

[They fight.]

Macbeth. Thou losest labour:
    As easy mayst thou the intrenchant air
    With thy keen sword impress, as make me bleed:
    Let fall thy blade on vulnerable crests;
    I bear a charmed life, which must not yield
    To one of woman born.
Macduff. Despair thy charm;
    And let the angel whom thou still hast serv'd
    Tell thee, Macduff was from his mother's womb
    Untimely ripp'd.

Macbeth. Accursed be that tongue that tells me so,
    For it hath cow'd my better part of man!
    And be these juggling fiends no more believ'd,
    That palter with us in a double sense;
    That keep the word of promise to our ear,
    And break it to our hope! – I'll not fight with thee.
Macduff. Then yield thee, coward,
    And live to be the show and gaze o' the time:
    We'll have thee, as our rarer monsters are,
    Painted upon a pole, and underwrit,
    "Here may you see the tyrant."
Macbeth. I will not yield,
    To kiss the ground before young Malcolm's feet,
    And to be baited with the rabble's curse.
    Though Birnam wood be come to Dunsinane,
    And thou oppos'd, being of no woman born,
    Yet I will try the last. Before my body
    I throw my warlike shield: lay on, Macduff;
    And damn'd be him that first cries, "Hold, enough!"

[Exeunt fighting.]

[Retreat. Flourish. Enter, with drum and colours, Malcolm, old
    Siward, Ross, Lennox, Angus, Caithness, Menteith, and Soldiers.

Malcolm. I would the friends we miss were safe arriv'd.
Siward. Some must go off; and yet, by these I see,
    So great a day as this is cheaply bought.
Malcolm. Macduff is missing, and your noble son.
Ross. Your son, my lord, has paid a soldier's debt:
    He only liv'd but till he was a man;
    The which no sooner had his prowess confirm'd
    In the unshrinking station where he fought,
    But like a man he died.
Siward. Then he is dead?
Fleance. Ay, and brought off the field: your cause of sorrow
    Must not be measur'd by his worth, for then
    It hath no end.
Siward. Had he his hurts before?
Ross. Ay, on the front.
Siward. Why then, God's soldier be he!

Had I as many sons as I have hairs,
I would not wish them to a fairer death:
And, so his knell is knoll'd.
Malcolm. He's worth more sorrow,
   And that I'll spend for him.
Siward. He's worth no more:
   They say he parted well, and paid his score:
   And so, God be with him! – Here comes newer comfort.

[*Re-enter* Macduff, *with* Macbeth's *head.*]

Macduff. Hail, king, for so thou art: behold, where stands
   The usurper's cursed head: the time is free:
   I see thee compass'd with thy kingdom's pearl
   That speak my salutation in their minds;
   Whose voices I desire aloud with mine, –
   Hail, King of Scotland!
All. Hail, King of Scotland!

[*Flourish.*]

Malcolm. We shall not spend a large expense of time
   Before we reckon with your several loves,
   And make us even with you. My thanes and kinsmen,
   Henceforth be earls, the first that ever Scotland
   In such an honour nam'd. What's more to do,
   Which would be planted newly with the time, –
   As calling home our exil'd friends abroad,
   That fled the snares of watchful tyranny;
   Producing forth the cruel ministers
   Of this dead butcher, and his fiend-like queen, –
   Who, as 'tis thought, by self and violent hands
   Took off her life; – this, and what needful else
   That calls upon us, by the grace of Grace,
   We will perform in measure, time, and place:
   So, thanks to all at once, and to each one,
   Whom we invite to see us crown'd at Scone.

[*Flourish. Exeunt.*]

20,000 Leagues Under the Sea by Jules Verne
A Christmas Carol by Charles Dickens
A Portrait of the Artist as a Young Man by James Joyce
A Princess of Mars by Edgar Rice Burroughs
A Room with a View by E. M. Forster
A Study in Scarlet by Arthur Conan Doyle
A Tale of Two Cities by Charles Dickens
Aesop's Fables by Aesop
Alice in Wonderland by Lewis Carroll
Anna Karenina by Leo Tolstoy
Anne of Green Gables by Lucy Maud Montgomery
Around the World in 80 Days by Jules Verne
Black Beauty by Anna Sewell
Bleak House by Charles Dickens
Candide by Voltaire
Common Sense by Thomas Paine
Crime and Punishment by Fyodor Dostoevsky
Don Quixote by Miguel de Cervantes
Dracula by Bram Stoker
Dubliners by James Joyce
Emma by Jane Austen
Far from the Madding Crowd by Thomas Hardy
Frankenstein by Mary Shelley
From the Earth to the Moon by Jules Verne
Great Expectations by Charles Dickens
Grimm's Fairy Tales by Jakob and Wilhelm Grimm
Gulliver's Travels by Jonathan Swift
Hamlet by William Shakespeare
Hard Times by Charles Dickens
Heart of Darkness by Joseph Conrad
Howards End by E. M. Forster
Jane Eyre by Charlotte Brontë
Journey to the Center of the Earth by Jules Verne
Kidnapped by Robert Louis Stevenson
Kim by Rudyard Kipling
Les Misérables by Victor Hugo
Little Men by Louisa May Alcott
Little Women by Louisa May Alcott
Macbeth by William Shakespeare
Madame Bovary by Gustave Flaubert
Mansfield Park by Jane Austen
Meditations by Marcus Aurelius
Middlemarch by George Eliot
Moby Dick by Herman Melville
My Ántonia by Willa Cather
Nicomachean Ethics by Aristotle